POTENTIAL EXPORTS AND NONTARIFF BARRIERS TO TRADE
BHUTAN NATIONAL STUDY

NOVEMBER 2021

 Creative Commons Attribution 3.0 IGO license (CC BY 3.0 IGO)

© 2021 Asian Development Bank
6 ADB Avenue, Mandaluyong City, 1550 Metro Manila, Philippines
Tel +63 2 8632 4444; Fax +63 2 8636 2444
www.adb.org

Some rights reserved. Published in 2021.

ISBN 978-92-9269-105-9 (print); 978-92-9269-106-6 (electronic); 978-92-9269-107-3 (ebook)
Publication Stock No. TCS210405-2
DOI: http://dx.doi.org/10.22617/TCS210405-2

The views expressed in this publication are those of the authors and do not necessarily reflect the views and policies of the Asian Development Bank (ADB) or its Board of Governors or the governments they represent.

ADB does not guarantee the accuracy of the data included in this publication and accepts no responsibility for any consequence of their use. The mention of specific companies or products of manufacturers does not imply that they are endorsed or recommended by ADB in preference to others of a similar nature that are not mentioned.

By making any designation of or reference to a particular territory or geographic area, or by using the term "country" in this document, ADB does not intend to make any judgments as to the legal or other status of any territory or area.

This work is available under the Creative Commons Attribution 3.0 IGO license (CC BY 3.0 IGO) https://creativecommons.org/licenses/by/3.0/igo/. By using the content of this publication, you agree to be bound by the terms of this license. For attribution, translations, adaptations, and permissions, please read the provisions and terms of use at https://www.adb.org/terms-use#openaccess.

This CC license does not apply to non-ADB copyright materials in this publication. If the material is attributed to another source, please contact the copyright owner or publisher of that source for permission to reproduce it. ADB cannot be held liable for any claims that arise as a result of your use of the material.

Please contact pubsmarketing@adb.org if you have questions or comments with respect to content, or if you wish to obtain copyright permission for your intended use that does not fall within these terms, or for permission to use the ADB logo.

Corrigenda to ADB publications may be found at http://www.adb.org/publications/corrigenda.

Note:
In this publication, "$" refers to United States dollars.

Cover design by Edith Creus.

 Printed on recycled paper

Contents

Tables and Figures — v

Acknowledgments — vi

Abbreviations — vii

Executive Summary — viii

Chapter 1 Introduction — 1
Background — 1
Objectives of the Study — 2
Brief Overview of Nontariff Measures in Bhutan — 2
Methodology of the Study — 3
Overview of the Study — 4

Chapter 2 Pattern of Trade with Other SASEC Countries — 6
Bhutan's Exports and Imports with Bangladesh — 10
Bhutan's Exports and Imports with India — 11
Bhutan's Exports and Imports with Nepal — 11

Chapter 3 Potential Exports Subject to Nontariff Barriers — 12
Potential Export Products from Bhutan to Bangladesh — 12
Potential Export Products from Bhutan to India — 14
Potential Export Products from Bhutan to Nepal — 15

Chapter 4 Overview of Sanitary and Phytosanitary and Technical Barriers to Trade in Bhutan — 17
The Sanitary and Phytosanitary Scenario — 17
Technical Barriers to Trade Scenario — 28

Chapter 5 Standards, Regulations, and Procedural Obstacles in the SASEC Countries That Impede Bhutan Import and Export Trade — 33
Impediments while Exporting to Bangladesh — 33
Impediments while Exporting to India — 36
Impediments while Exporting to Nepal — 37

Chapter 6 Prioritized Recommendations for Action — 39
Legislation and Regulatory Frameworks — 39
Institutional Frameworks — 40
Infrastructure Development — 41

Chapter 7 Conclusion — 43

Appendixes
1. Top 10 Export and Import Products between Bhutan and Other SASEC Countries — 44
2. Potential Export Items from Bhutan to Other SASEC Countries — 47
3. Existing Gaps in Standards and Regulations, Sanitary and Phytosanitary and Technical Barriers to Trade Measures, and Procedural Obstacles — 60
4. Products for Exemption of Customs Duty — 85
5. Stakeholders and Contributors to the Bhutan National Diagnostic Study — 92

References — 96

Tables and Figures

Tables

1	Sanitary and Phytosanitary-Related Infrastructure in Bhutan	22
2	Trade Entry and Exit Points in India for Import to and Export from Bhutan	23
3	Identified Trade Routes for Bhutan and Bangladesh	24
4	Infrastructure and Human Resource of Laboratory Facilities	27
5	Impediments while Exporting to Bangladesh	34
6	Impediments while Exporting to India	36
7	Impediments while Exporting to Nepal	38
A1.1	Top 10 Export Products to Bangladesh in 2015	44
A1.2	Top 10 Import Products from Bangladesh to Bhutan in 2015	44
A1.3	Top 10 Export Products to India in 2015 (Excluding Electricity)	45
A1.4	Top 10 Import Products from India to Bhutan in 2015	45
A1.5	Top 10 Export Products to Nepal in 2015	46
A1.6	Top 10 Import Products from Nepal to Bhutan in 2015	46
A2.1	Potential and Existing Export Products from Bhutan to Bangladesh	47
A2.2	Potential and Existing Export Products from Bhutan to India	51
A2.3	Potential and Existing Export Products from Bhutan to Nepal	52
A3.1	Existing Gaps in the Bangladesh Market	60
A3.2	Existing Gaps in Indian Market	74
A3.3	Existing Gaps in Nepal Market	77
A4.1	Exportable Products from Bhutan to Bangladesh	85
A4.2	Exportable Products from Bangladesh to Bhutan	88
A4.3	Proposed List of 15 Products for Exemption of Customs Duty	91
A4.4	Additional Products for Exemption of Customs Duty	91

Figures

1	Filters Applied to Identify Potential Export Products	5
2	Exports of Bhutan to SASEC Countries	6
3	Imports from SASEC Countries to Bhutan	7
4	Share of Bhutan Exports to SASEC and to India in Total Exports	7
5	Total Imports from SASEC Compared with Imports from India	8
6	Bhutan Trade Balance with Bangladesh	8
7	Bhutan Trade Balance with India	9
8	Bhutan Trade Balance with Nepal	9
9	Potential Export Products from Bhutan to Bangladesh	13
10	Potential Export Products from Bhutan to India	14
11	Potential Export Products from Bhutan to Nepal	15

Acknowledgments

Sonam Tobgay, national consultant for Bhutan under the South Asia Subregional Economic Cooperation (SASEC) Trade Facilitation Program, prepared the national diagnostic report, supported by the Asian Development Bank (ADB) and in close collaboration with the Bhutan Sanitary and Phytosanitary and Technical Barriers to Trade Core Group. The report was designed jointly by the Trade and Investment Division of the United Nations Economic and Social Commission for Asia and the Pacific, and ADB, which also serves as the SASEC Secretariat.

The project team gratefully recognizes the support, guidance, and contributions from the start of Namgay Wangchuk, director general, Bhutan Agriculture and Food Regulatory Agency, Ministry of Agriculture and Forests; and Sonam Tenzin, director, Department of Trade, Ministry of Economic Affairs. Sonam Phuntsho, director general, Bhutan Standards Bureau, also provided valuable recommendations and inputs.

The Bhutan Sanitary and Phytosanitary and Technical Barriers to Trade Core Group gave strong technical and contextual advice for the preparation of the national diagnostic report: Passang W. Norbu, chief, Social Forestry Division, Department of Forests and Park Services, Ministry of Agriculture and Forests; Zecko, chief trade officer, Department of Trade, Ministry of Economic Affairs; N. P. Dahal, principal livestock officer, Department of Livestock, Ministry of Agriculture and Forests; Pema Thinley, plant protection officer, National Plant Protection Centre, Department of Agriculture, Ministry of Agriculture and Forests; Yeshi Dorji, senior research officer, Bhutan Chamber of Commerce and Industry; Tshewang Norbu, marketing officer, Department of Agricultural Marketing and Cooperatives, Ministry of Agriculture and Forests; and Tshering Yeshi, general secretary, Bhutan Exporters Association, Phuentsholing. The study also benefited from consultations with Phub Tshering, secretary general, Bhutan Chamber of Commerce and Industry. Crucial insights were received through rich interactions with various commodity associations and exporting firms in Bhutan.

Rose McKenzie, senior regional cooperation specialist, ADB, oversaw the preparation of the national diagnostic report, and Selim Raihan, international consultant, ADB, provided excellent substantive guidance throughout the process. Achyut Bhandari, national consultant on regional cooperation, ADB; Sonam Dema, SASEC program coordinator, ADB; and Phuntsho Wangdi, national trade facilitation consultant, ADB, helped organize the national-level consultations and meetings, and facilitated government input and feedback on the report. Roble P. Velasco-Rosenheim, international consultant, ADB, edited the report.

Abbreviations

ADB	Asian Development Bank
BAFRA	Bhutan Agriculture and Food Regulatory Authority
BSB	Bhutan Standards Bureau
BSTI	Bangladesh Standards and Testing Institution
DRC	Department of Revenue and Customs
FSSAI	Food Safety Standard Authority of India
GMO	genetically modified organism
GST	goods and services tax
HS	Harmonized System
IEC	International Electrotechnical Commission
ISO	International Organization for Standardization
NFTL	National Food Testing Laboratory
NML	National Metrology Laboratory
NTTFC	National Transport and Trade Facilitation Committee
SAARC	South Asian Association for Regional Cooperation
SARSO	South Asian Regional Standards Organization
SASEC	South Asia Subregional Economic Cooperation
SPS	sanitary and phytosanitary
TBT	technical barrier to trade

Executive Summary

The South Asia Subregional Economic Cooperation (SASEC) program brings together Bangladesh, Bhutan, India, Maldives, Myanmar, Nepal, and Sri Lanka in a project-based partnership that aims to promote regional prosperity, improve economic opportunities, and build a better quality of life for the people of the subregion. Under its broader mandate and the SASEC Trade Facilitation Strategic Framework, 2014–2018, the SASEC program provides targeted support to improve the efficiency of intraregional trade. The Asian Development Bank (ADB) supports the SASEC partnership with technical assistance and financing to overcome key barriers to trade. Against this backdrop, the SASEC member countries, jointly with ADB, have prepared a series of diagnostic studies to help policy makers and the private sector improve trade ties and efficiency, specifically in the area of sanitary and phytosanitary (SPS) measures and technical barriers to trade (TBTs).

This series of diagnostic studies focuses on how SPS measures and TBTs affect the efficient movement of goods across the SASEC subregion. It looks to how policy makers and private sector stakeholders can collaborate on reducing bottlenecks and drive economic prosperity across the subregion. The series comprises a national study each for Bangldesh, Bhutan, India, Maldives, Nepal, and Sri Lanka, as well as a subregional study that collates key findings and identifies potential areas for collaboration across SASEC members.

This national study for Bhutan uses a research methodology that is aligned with the studies prepared for the other SASEC members. The study examines trade dynamics between Bhutan and its major trade partners in SASEC—India, Bangladesh, and, to a lesser extent, Nepal—with the goals of (i) identifying export products from Bhutan that could potentially be traded more between the SASEC members, (ii) indicating SPS and TBT issues that restrict trade, and (iii) providing actionable recommendations on how to overcome these issues.

The introduction describes the objectives and methodology used to prepare the study. The methodology centers on identifying potential export products that have not been traded (or are traded minimally) because of the application of SPS and TBT measures. Drawing on the methodology, the study identifies potential export products by reviewing domestic trade data and applying a six-step filtering process. It also draws on desk research, field visits, and interviews with stakeholders across the public and private sectors to provide a robust picture of domestic and regional barriers to trade.

Chapter 2 presents Bhutan's trade patterns with Bangladesh, India, and Nepal. Trade with other SASEC countries represents more than 90% of Bhutan's total trade, and trade with India about 90% of its trade with SASEC. Trade with India constitutes about 90%

of Bhutan's total exports and 95% of its imports, and in 2015, Bhutan suffered from a significant trade deficit of about $400 million with India. The dominance of trade with India is largely attributed to favorable free trade and transit agreements between the two countries. Trade with Bangladesh is favorable, and dominated by Bhutanese cardamom and fruit exports, while trade with Nepal has been modest in the past. Imports from Nepal are limited to precious metals (silver) and silk textiles, with an aggregate value of $0.2 million, and exports comprise gypsum ($0.942 million) and coal ($0.119 million).

Chapter 3 builds on the description of Bhutan's trade profile by identifying exports that could be increased through collaboration to overcome SPS and TBT constraints. The products were selected through a six-stage filtering process, which examines different export opportunities to Bangladesh, India, and Nepal. The study identifies a total of 53 potential export products to Bangladesh, with a total export value of $116 million. Products on the list are not currently exported from Bhutan to Bangladesh, but could be introduced in line with decreased SPS and TBT constraining measures. Bangladesh currently imports these products from other countries, with total imports valued at $1,281 million. For India, the study identifies 13 potential products constituting a total value of $16 million that Bhutan exports to other countries but only nominally to India. India's annual imports of these products come to about $2,250 million. With respect to Nepal, the study finds 101 potential products with a total export value of $278 million that Bhutan exports to other countries but only negligibly to Nepal. On the other hand, Nepal imports these same 101 products worth $645 million from other countries but not from Bhutan. The study proceeds to analyze SPS and TBT issues that restrict Bhutanese exports of these goods, both as a result of domestic factors and restrictions or inefficiencies imposed by its trade partners.

To begin identifying approaches to scale up efficient trade, Chapter 4 provides an overview of SPS and TBT legislation, institutional frameworks, and related infrastructure constraints in Bhutan. It describes the various laws that govern food safety and trade, as well as the different organizations responsible for establishing and enforcing policies, setting standards, and providing certification. Chapter 4 also notes the gaps in terms of legislation, institutional frameworks, and SPS- and TBT-related infrastructure in Bhutan against international best practices. These constraints broadly include legislative frameworks that provide for overlapping roles and responsibilities among different agencies; lack of SPS standards for many consumer items; lack of recognition of Bhutanese product certification by importing countries; insufficient SPS- and TBT-related infrastructure, including laboratories and testing equipment; and limited domestic technical capacity and human resources.

Chapter 5 identifies standards, regulations, and procedural obstacles in SASEC countries that impede trade of the items identified in Chapter 3, highlighting SPS and TBT measures applied by the importing countries (Bangladesh, India, and Nepal) and Bhutan. Chapter 5 looks specifically at standards and regulations as they relate to certification requirements, accreditation of laboratories, and associated barriers to Bhutanese product clearance into other markets. It also identifies key procedural obstacles that affect Bhutanese exporters, such as inefficient banking procedures, infrastructure gaps, and logistical inefficiencies that increase the costs of trade and restrict Bhutanese exports into other SASEC markets.

Chapter 6 lays out practical recommendations for the public and private sectors, grouped under (i) the legislative and regulatory framework environment, (ii) institutional frameworks, and (iii) SPS- and TBT-related infrastructure status and gaps. Key recommendations include the following:

(i) updating legislation and regulatory frameworks for standard setting, certification, laboratory testing, enforcement, and compliance;
(ii) securing international accreditation of SPS and TBT analytical laboratories;
(iii) strengthening and expediting collaboration between national SPS and TBT agencies and subregional bodies, and moving toward developing mutual recognition arrangements;
(iv) enhancing SPS and TBT dialogue and diplomacy with other SASEC countries;
(v) designating clear institutional mandates to avoid duplication and overlap;
(vi) building sustainable institutional skills and technical capacity;
(vii) increasing access to SPS and TBT information for the public and private sectors;
(viii) providing adequate SPS and TBT laboratory facilities and equipment, including potential private sector investment; and
(ix) exploring opportunities to develop subregional infrastructure and facility networks.

Overall, the study seeks to provide policy makers and private sector stakeholders with a clear image of the opportunities that exist to enhance Bhutan's trade across the SASEC subregion, and to provide actionable recommendations on how to reduce SPS and TBT bottlenecks that currently affect trade.

Chapter 1
Introduction

Background

The Kingdom of Bhutan is situated in the Himalayan mountain range and is home to about 730,000 people. Although Bhutan is on the United Nations' list of least developed countries, it has made tremendous progress since 2010 to drive socioeconomic development, and expects to graduate from the list in 2023. Strengthening trade ties with subregional neighbors can drive more inclusive and sustainable growth as the country continues its efforts to increase exports and diversify trade.

Sanitary and phytosanitary (SPS) measures aim to ensure food safety and the healthy cultivation, trade, and consumption of plants and animals. Technical barriers to trade (TBTs) may include regulations, product standards, and certification procedures intended to support safety and quality assurance, but that can also create unintended barriers to trade. Viewed together, SPS measures and trade regulations are essential for safeguarding national security, but can also generate inefficiencies in the movement of goods and services. In the context of Bhutanese trade with members of the South Asia Subregional Economic Cooperation (SASEC) partnership, SPS and TBT issues restrict the volumes of potential exports.[1] As such, identifying the core SPS and TBT issues and solutions will support Bhutan's economic development and more robust participation in regional and subregional markets.

Since 2002, members of the SASEC partnership have shared a common vision of boosting intraregional trade and cooperation in South Asia while also developing connectivity and trade with Southeast Asia, the People's Republic of China, and broader global markets. The SASEC partnership has clear potential to increase intraregional trade between and among its members. However, infrastructural, SPS, and TBT bottlenecks persist, contributing to high costs of doing business and suboptimal trade volumes. Trade practices in Bhutan and the subregion still encounter challenges, including

(i) minimal harmonization of nontariff barriers;
(ii) limited computerization and automated systems;

---

[1] SASEC members are Bangladesh, Bhutan, India, Maldives, Myanmar, Nepal, and Sri Lanka.

(iii) lack of modern customs procedures such as Harmonized System (HS) code discrepancies,[2] and lengthy documentation with manual processing that is required in numerous copies; and

(iv) poor testing and laboratory facilities that are not recognized by regional and international standards.

In 2013, SASEC members initiated regional dialogue on SPS and TBT nontariff measures, and in 2014 endorsed the formal inclusion of this agenda as a component of the SASEC Trade Facilitation Strategic Framework, 2014–2018.[3] In 2016, the Asian Development Bank (ADB) initiated consultations in six SASEC countries and launched a national diagnostic study process, led by groups of public and private sector stakeholders in each of the SASEC countries.[4]

Objectives of the Study

This diagnostic study seeks to analyze export-related SPS and TBT constraints in the context of Bhutanese trade with other SASEC countries, and seeks potential paths to overcome them. The study is intended to help

(i) identify specific products that have potential for export from Bhutan, yet that are subject to SPS and TBT measures of importing SASEC countries;

(ii) carry out a diagnostic on SPS and TBT measures imposed on the identified products;

(iii) identify current SPS and TBT infrastructure constraints and share recommendations for future investments to address them;

(iv) prioritize national capacity building requirements in the areas of standards and regulations.

Brief Overview of Nontariff Measures in Bhutan

The majority of imports into Bhutan must be authorized by an import license issued by the Department of Revenue and Customs (DRC) under the supervision of the Ministry of Economic Affairs.[5] While imports entering Bhutan by air transport do not require an import license, they are subject to standard SPS and TBT measures and DRC regulations. All consignments originating from countries other than India and entering by road—including those entering Bhutan by road transit passing through India—need an import license. Import licenses are issued free of charge and have up to 1 year of validity. The Bhutan

---

[2] The Harmonized Commodity Description and Coding System of the World Customs Organization, referred to as "Harmonized System" or simply "HS," is a multipurpose international product nomenclature. More than 5,000 commodity groups are identified by a six digit code, arranged in a legal and logical structure; see http://www.wcoomd.org/en/topics/nomenclature/overview/what-is-the-harmonized-system.aspx.
[3] Asian Development Bank (ADB). 2014. *SASEC Trade Facilitation Strategic Framework, 2014–2018*. Manila.
[4] Myanmar joined SASEC in 2017 and was not included in the SPS and TBT diagnostic initiative.
[5] S. Raihan, M.A. Khan, and S. Quoreshi. 2014. *NTMs in South Asia: Assessment and Analysis*. Kathmandu: South Asian Association for Regional Cooperation (SAARC) Trade Promotion Network.

Agriculture and Food Regulatory Authority (BAFRA) monitors all imported food, plant, and livestock products entering Bhutan for safety and quality in line with adequate rules, regulations, and standard protocols.[6]

All Bhutanese exports must be channeled through a license holder issued by the DRC. Bhutanese exports are required to pass through approved and notified exit and entry points of customs offices located in border towns. Accordingly, all SPS-related inspection and testing requirements are a major reason for such port of entry and exit of consignments.

Bhutanese agricultural exports, including seeds, rice, *Cordyceps sinensis*, and fresh fruits and vegetables, require certification from BAFRA to facilitate transactions with importers in Bangladesh and India. Mandatory grading and sorting is also carried out, and relevant certificates are issued for tangerines, as well as for pebbles and boulders for export. Additionally, traders must obtain a certificate of origin for exports.

Bhutan must use Indian roads and seaports (primarily Kolkata) for transshipment of its products to other countries. For transshipments to Bangladesh, Bhutanese exports must use special ports of entry as per the requirements of relevant trade protocols between India (Changrabandha land port) and Bangladesh (Burimari land port). Likewise, Haldia and Kolkata seaports are used for Bhutanese exports to markets that are not members of the South Asian Association for Regional Cooperation (SAARC), such as Australia; Hong Kong, China; the Republic of Korea; and Singapore.

Methodology of the Study

The SASEC countries agreed on common terms of reference and methodology for the six national diagnostic studies, presented in the data capture and analysis of Appendixes 1–3. The methodology was designed to accommodate minor adjustments to reflect national priorities and preferences.

Data Sources and Selectivity

The export value of Bhutan and Bhutan's exports to other countries are taken from the partner country's global import data for specific products is sourced from the United Nations Comtrade database.[7]

Annual data from *Bhutan Trade Statistics* for 2011–2015 were analyzed at the six-digit HS level to determine the following for each potential product:

(i) the average export value of the product from Bhutan,
(ii) the average unit value of export of the product from Bhutan to the importing country, and
(iii) the average share of Bhutan's export to the identified importing country.

---

[6] Government of Bhutan, Ministry of Agriculture and Forests, BAFRA. 2015. *Gist of Achievements, August 2000–June 2014*. Thimphu.
[7] United Nations. United Nations Comtrade database (accessed 2017–2018).

Similarly, United Nations Comtrade data were analyzed to determine the following:

(i) the average import value by the importing countries (India, Bangladesh, and Nepal) from the global market; and
(ii) the average unit of import by the importing countries (India, Bangladesh, and Nepal).

According to all data sources, Bhutanese trade with Maldives and Sri Lanka is negligible, and this national diagnostic study therefore focuses only on potential trade cooperation between Bhutan and Bangladesh, India, and Nepal.

Data Processing

Averages refer to product-specific data on exports and imports. The average unit value of exports and imports is calculated for 2011–2015 and follows the steps below, where

(i) average unit value of exports of Bhutan = export value of Bhutan ÷ quantity exported;
(ii) average unit cost of imports by importing country = import value by importing country ÷ quantity imported;
(iii) average share of imports of importing country from Bhutan = importing country imports from Bhutan ÷ total imports of importing country; and
(iv) average share of exports from Bhutan to importing country = Bhutan's exports to importing ÷ total exports of Bhutan.

Identifying Potential Export Products

Potential export products were determined by applying the filtering process outlined in Figure 1.

Qualitative Review and Consultations to Identify Barriers

The study team interviewed key stakeholders and conducted consultations with officials from BAFRA, the Bhutan Standards Bureau (BSB), the DRC, the Department of Trade, municipal authorities, industry associations, and exporters.[8] The study team conducted two field visits to interact with stakeholders—including exporters, food processors, industry owners, and entrepreneurs—and to solicit their views and experience with trade partners during export and import procedures.

Overview of the Study

The Bhutan national diagnostic study attempts to identify both existing and potential export products from Bhutan to other SASEC countries that remain subject to SPS and TBT measures. Chapter 1 provides the background and objectives of the study.

---

[8] A complete list of government agencies, private sector companies, and individuals who contributed to the study is in Appendix 5.

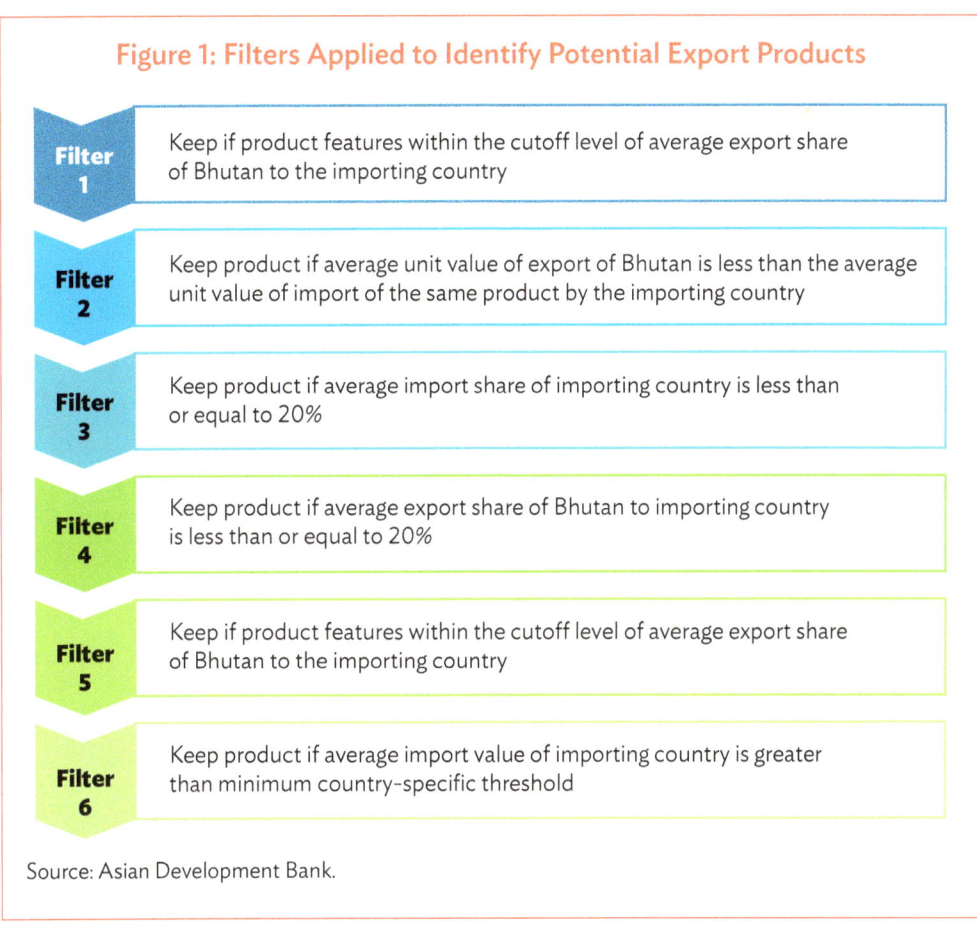

Figure 1: Filters Applied to Identify Potential Export Products

Filter 1: Keep if product features within the cutoff level of average export share of Bhutan to the importing country

Filter 2: Keep product if average unit value of export of Bhutan is less than the average unit value of import of the same product by the importing country

Filter 3: Keep product if average import share of importing country is less than or equal to 20%

Filter 4: Keep product if average export share of Bhutan to importing country is less than or equal to 20%

Filter 5: Keep if product features within the cutoff level of average export share of Bhutan to the importing country

Filter 6: Keep product if average import value of importing country is greater than minimum country-specific threshold

Source: Asian Development Bank.

Chapter 2 outlines Bhutan's trade patterns with other SASEC countries to help identify underlying bottlenecks to trade, focusing on SPS- and TBT-related barriers. Chapter 3 identifies products that have export potential from Bhutan to other SASEC countries, but which are restricted by SPS and TBT measures of the importing country. Chapter 4 provides an overview of the SPS and TBT scenarios in Bhutan, covering legal, institutional, and infrastructural dimensions, as well as the gaps in current national legislation, and between local practice and international best practice. Chapter 5 identifies standards, regulations, and procedural obstacles in the SASEC countries that impede trade of the potential exports identified in Chapter 3. Chapter 5 also recognizes major export markets by product and the types of SPS and TBT changes required to enhance trade. Chapter 6 provides recommendations on how to facilitate trade by addressing restrictive SPS and TBT measures, including proposed actions under legal frameworks, institutional capacity building, infrastructure development, and human resource management. Conclusions of the study are described in Chapter 7.

Chapter 2
Pattern of Trade with Other SASEC Countries

Bhutan is a signatory to the Agreement on the South Asian Free Trade Area and, as a least developed country, benefits from special and differential treatment, including enhanced market access through smaller sensitive lists in some South Asian Free Trade Area countries,[9] and less stringent rules of origin.[10] Trade with SASEC countries represents more than 90% of Bhutan's total trade, and trade with India about 90% of its total trade with SASEC (Figures 2 and 3). While Bhutan's exports to Bangladesh have risen gradually, reaching $28 million in 2015, imports from SASEC countries, excluding India, remain low.

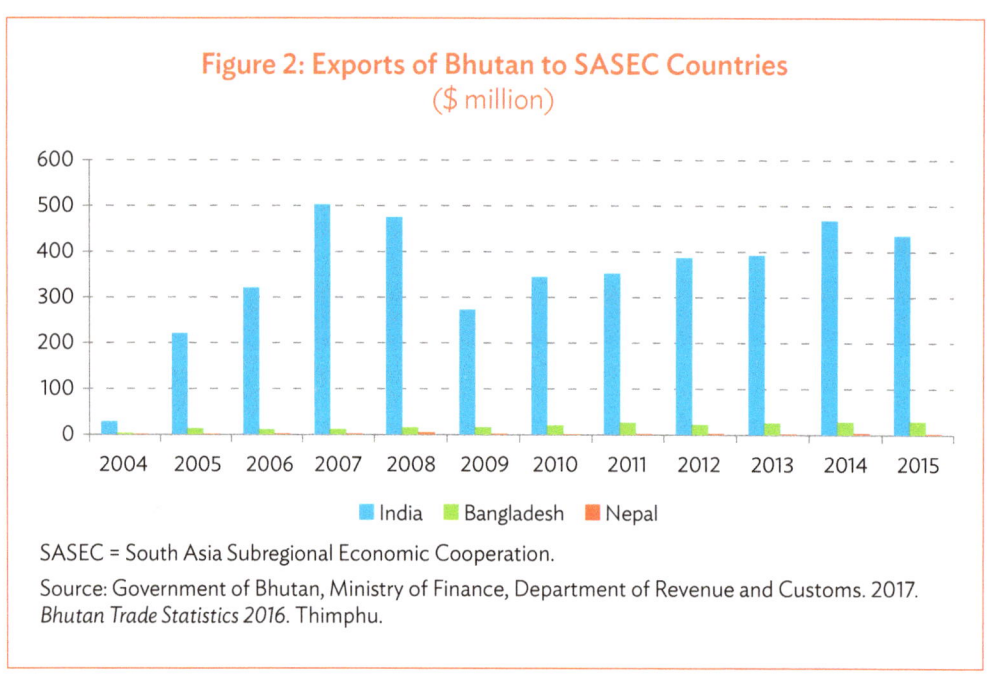

Figure 2: Exports of Bhutan to SASEC Countries ($ million)

SASEC = South Asia Subregional Economic Cooperation.
Source: Government of Bhutan, Ministry of Finance, Department of Revenue and Customs. 2017. *Bhutan Trade Statistics 2016*. Thimphu.

---

[9] The South Asian Free Trade Area sensitive list allows each participating country to maintain a sensitive list of products that remain outside of the trade liberalization process and are not subject to tariff concessions.
[10] World Bank. 2004 Agreement on South Asian Free Trade Area.

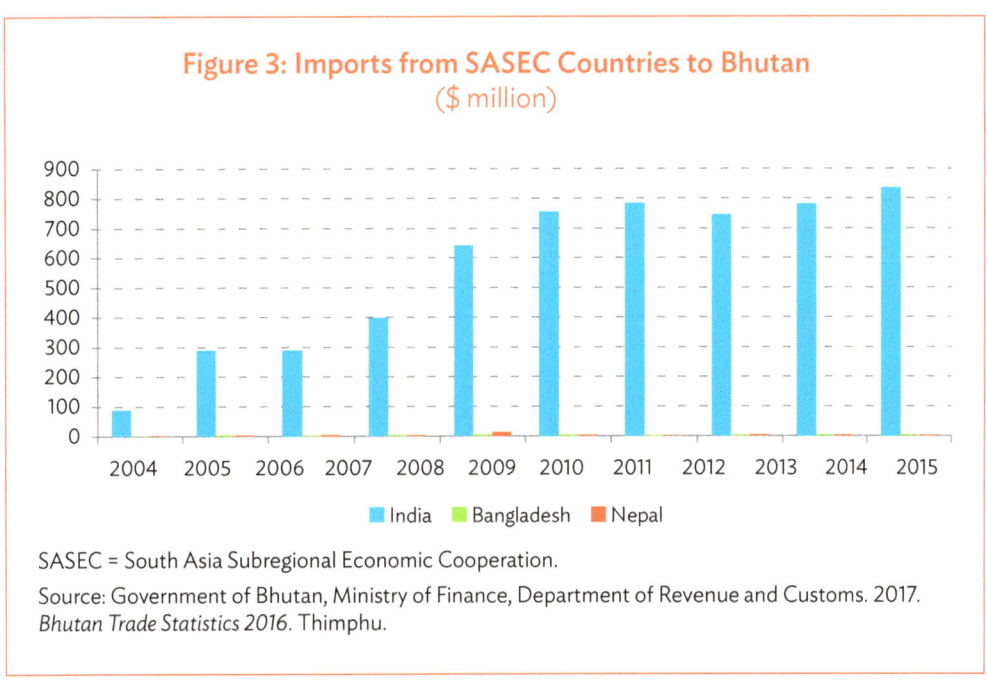

Figure 3: Imports from SASEC Countries to Bhutan ($ million)

SASEC = South Asia Subregional Economic Cooperation.
Source: Government of Bhutan, Ministry of Finance, Department of Revenue and Customs. 2017. *Bhutan Trade Statistics 2016*. Thimphu.

Figures 4 and 5 show the importance of India as Bhutan's main trading partner: Bhutan's total exports to the SASEC subregion in 2015, 91.2% went to India. Similarly, 79.3% of Bhutanese imports in 2015 came from India. Bhutan's exports to India constitute mainly hydroelectricity, while the bulk of imports comprise diesel fuel, essential goods, automobiles, and services of Indian laborers utilized in the construction sector.

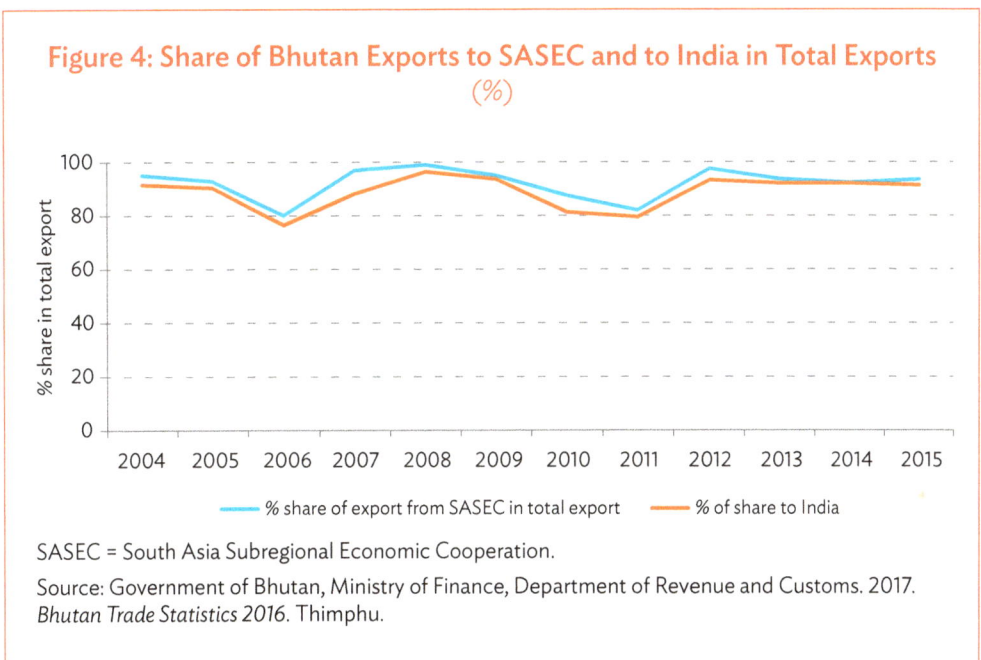

Figure 4: Share of Bhutan Exports to SASEC and to India in Total Exports (%)

SASEC = South Asia Subregional Economic Cooperation.
Source: Government of Bhutan, Ministry of Finance, Department of Revenue and Customs. 2017. *Bhutan Trade Statistics 2016*. Thimphu.

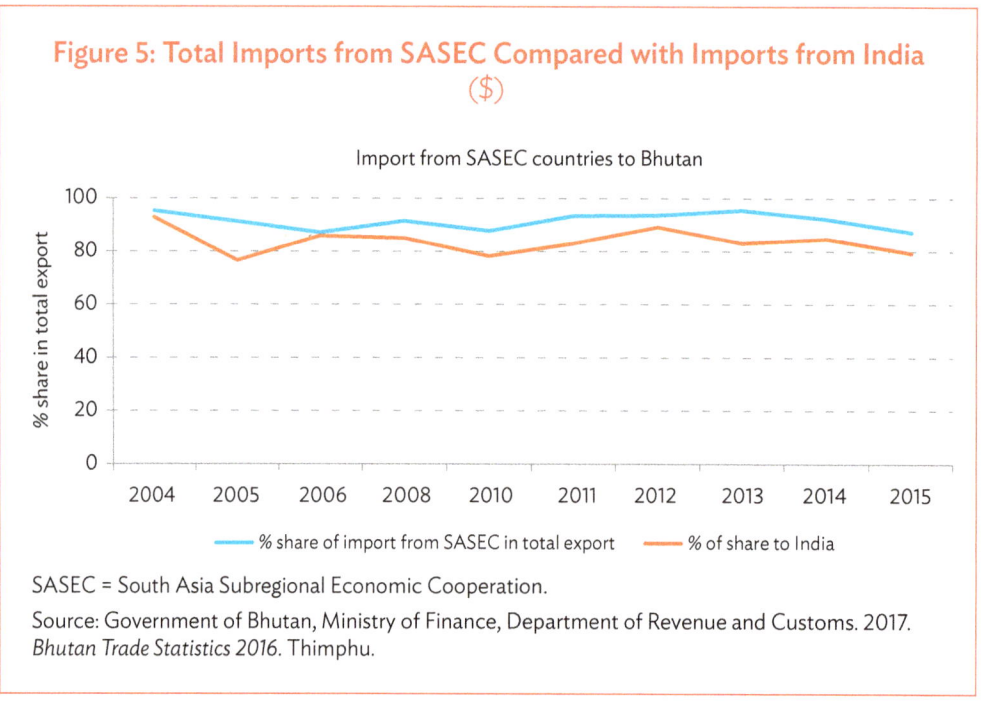

Figure 5: Total Imports from SASEC Compared with Imports from India ($)

SASEC = South Asia Subregional Economic Cooperation.
Source: Government of Bhutan, Ministry of Finance, Department of Revenue and Customs. 2017. *Bhutan Trade Statistics 2016*. Thimphu.

During 2012–2015, Bhutan's trade balance with India, Bangladesh, and Nepal indicated favorable conditions with Bangladesh and an increasing export trend. The situation was reversed with India, however, where imports from India into Bhutan starting to rise in 2010 (Figures 6–8).

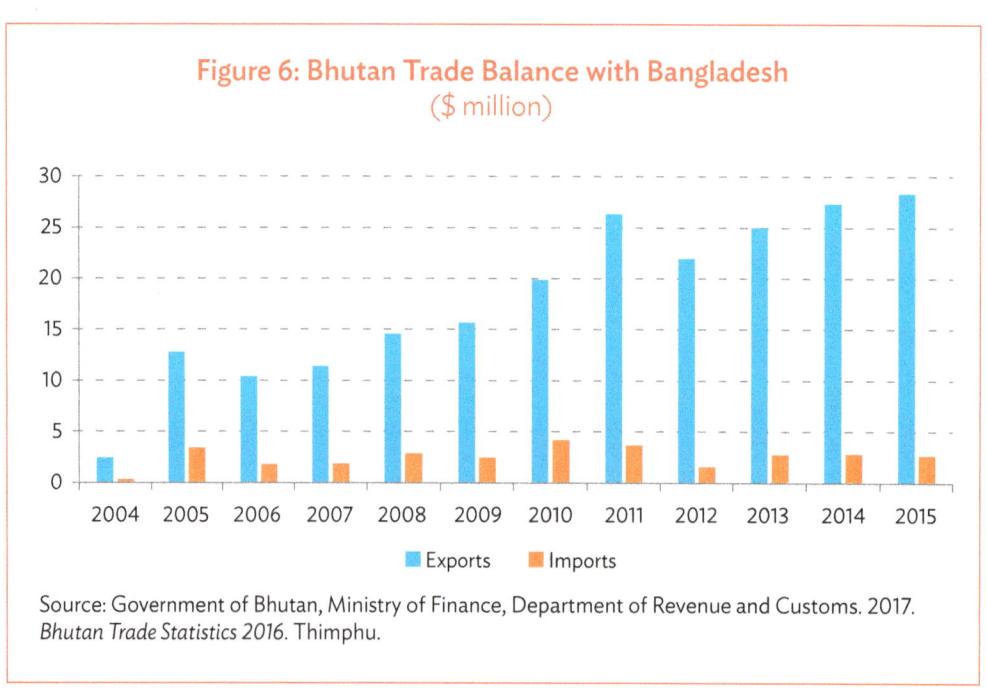

Figure 6: Bhutan Trade Balance with Bangladesh ($ million)

Source: Government of Bhutan, Ministry of Finance, Department of Revenue and Customs. 2017. *Bhutan Trade Statistics 2016*. Thimphu.

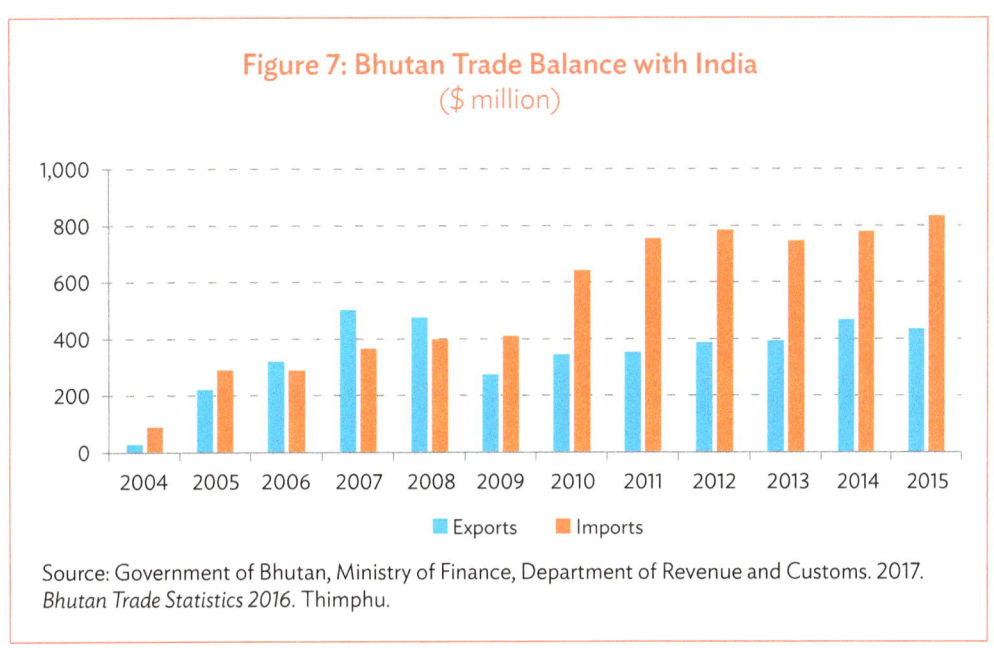

Figure 7: Bhutan Trade Balance with India
($ million)

Source: Government of Bhutan, Ministry of Finance, Department of Revenue and Customs. 2017. *Bhutan Trade Statistics 2016*. Thimphu.

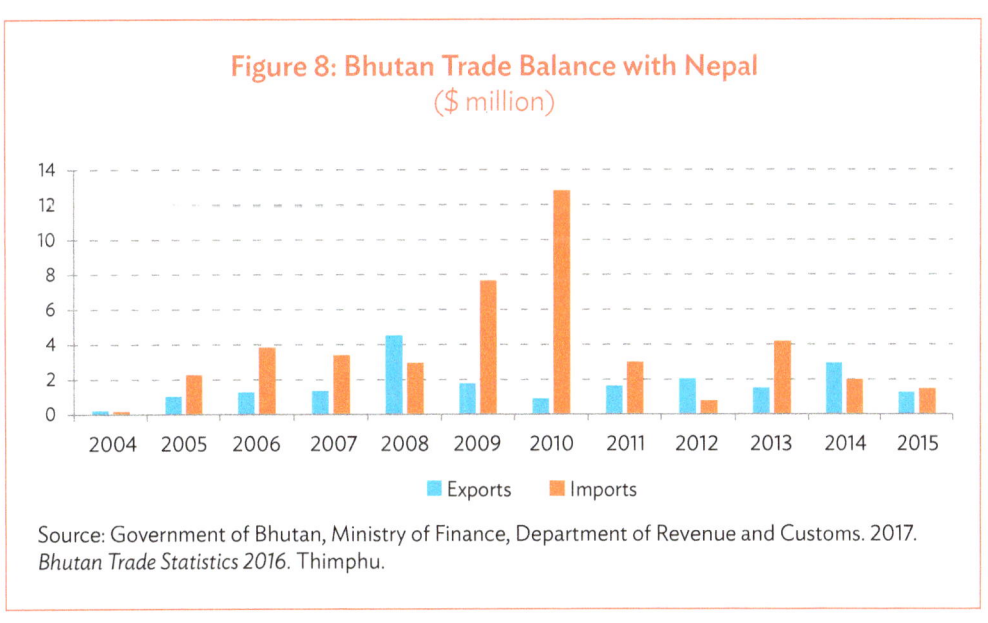

Figure 8: Bhutan Trade Balance with Nepal
($ million)

Source: Government of Bhutan, Ministry of Finance, Department of Revenue and Customs. 2017. *Bhutan Trade Statistics 2016*. Thimphu.

Trade dominance with India can be largely attributed to the Agreement on Trade, Commerce and Transit between the Royal Government of Bhutan and the Government of the Republic of India, which lays out the terms of free trade and commerce between the two countries.[11] It notes that Bhutan may impose nontariff restrictions on the entry into Bhutan of certain goods of Indian origin as may be needed to protect Bhutanese industries.

---

[11] Government of Bhutan, Ministry of Economic Affairs. 2006. *Agreement on Trade, Commerce and Transit between the Royal Government of Bhutan and the Government of the Republic of India*. Thimphu.

The proximity to markets in India—such as the border towns of the state of West Bengal—for both exports and imports is another contributing factor. Further, trade with India is conducted in Indian rupees, which are convertible at a 1:1 ratio to the Bhutanese ngultrum. Bhutan has been suffering from adverse balance of payments leading to Indian rupee shortages, as a result of the trimming down of imports (Figures 6–8). The annual report of the Royal Monetary Authority of Bhutan, 2015–2016 indicated a widening Bhutanese trade deficit, from $288 million in 2012 to $436 million in 2016, while the current account deficit increased from 25.2% of gross domestic product in 2015 to 29.8% in 2016.[12]

Bangladesh has encouraged trade with Bhutan by introducing a list of 18 Bhutanese products that are granted duty-free access to the Bangladesh market.[13] However, to make the duty-free list more robust, Bhutan has requested that Bangladesh revise the list and change the products.[14] Other export products of interest to Bhutan are protected with high tariffs, including mineral water (89.8%), Portland cement (89.8%), bars of iron (88.9%), and fruit juices (58.8%).

Bhutan provides fiscal incentives to select sectors, including mining; hotels and tourism; cottage, small, and medium-sized industries; and educational and health establishments. However, the question remains whether Bhutan has the productive capacity and the comparative advantage to boost exports in potential sectors while also reshaping high-value and low-volume sectors to carve a niche market, considering high transaction costs and scattered production facilities. The introduction of these fiscal incentives may help achieve targets on import substitution and export promotion, though no empirical review has been conducted on the probable impact of such incentives.[15]

Bhutan's Exports and Imports with Bangladesh

Trade with Bangladesh in 2015 was favorable for the top 10 products, dominated by cardamom exports at $8.57 million and followed by oranges at $6.77 million and limestone and other calcareous stone at $4.73 million (Appendix 1, Table A1.1). Total Bhutanese exports to Bangladesh of the top 10 products were valued at almost $25 million and represented close to 89.63% of total exports to Bangladesh. The top 10 import items into Bhutan from Bangladesh in 2015 included steel and aluminum furniture, garments, processed fruit juices, and selected pharmaceutical products (Appendix 1, Table A1.2). Imports from Bangladesh were relatively low in value, with each of the top 10 import groups showing less than a total worth of $400,000.

---

[12] Government of Bhutan, Royal Monetary Authority. 2017 *Annual Report, 2015–2016*. Thimphu.
[13] Government of Bangladesh, Export Promotion Bureau. Market Access Facilities.
[14] Government of Bhutan, Ministry of Foreign Affairs. 2017. News release. 19 April. See Appendix 4 for details on identified duty-free products.
[15] Government of Bhutan, Ministry of Finance. 2000. *Sales Tax, Customs and Excise Act of the Kingdom of Bhutan, 2000*. Thimphu; and Government of Bhutan, Ministry of Finance. 2001. *Income Tax Act of the Kingdom of Bhutan, 2001*. Thimphu.

Bhutan's Exports and Imports with India

Among the top 10 commodity exports from Bhutan to India in 2015 were ferrosilicon at $95.57 million, cement at $38.84 million, and semi-finished iron at $27.33 million (Appendix 1, Table A1.3). Bhutan's main export to India is hydroelectricity, with a total value of $189.44 million in 2015; however, electricity is outside the scope of the national diagnostic study because of its unique export characteristics.[16] In the agriculture sector, key Bhutanese exports included semi-milled rice at $17.32 million and bovine meat at $8.01 million (Appendix 1, Table A1.4). Imports from India included all essential consumer goods, automobiles, diesel fuel, and cooking gas; and were dominated by light oil, hydraulic turbines, and motor spirits.

Bhutan's Exports and Imports with Nepal

Trade with Nepal remained minimal in 2015. Among the top exports to Nepal was gypsum (worth $0.942 million), coal (worth $0.119 million), and coke and semi-coke (worth $0.013 million) (Appendix 1, Table A1.5). Top imports from Nepal were limited to precious metal (silverware) and silk brocade textiles, valued collectively at $0.14 million; toilet soap at $0.05 million; and prepared food items at $0.03 million (Appendix 1, Table A1.6).

---

[16] Government of Bhutan, Ministry of Finance, DRC. *Bhutan Trade Statistics 2016*. Thimphu.

Chapter 3
Potential Exports Subject to Nontariff Barriers

The following chapter identifies potential exports from Bhutan to Bangladesh, India, and Nepal using the six-step filtering process and based on data from the Bhutan Trade Statistics and the United Nations Comtrade database.

Potential Export Products from Bhutan to Bangladesh

The study identified a total of 1,505 potential products based on data for 2011–2015. Applying the filtering process, the following products were identified for export to Bangladesh:

(i) filter 1 identified 877 products, reduced to 341 after removing duplicates;
(ii) filter 2 identified 275 products;
(iii) filter 3 identified 265 products;
(iv) filter 4 identified 252 products;
(v) filter 5 identified 53 products with an average export value from Bhutan to Bangladesh of at least $100,000; and
(vi) filter 6 identified 53 products with an average import value into Bangladesh from Bhutan of less than $100,000.

Figure 9 shows the 53 identified potential export products from Bhutan to Bangladesh grouped by two-digit HS code. Under HS chapter 25, Bhutan's annual exports surpass $37.4 million, constituting mainly gypsum, cement clinkers, Portland cement, and plasters consisting of calcined gypsum. Base metals and articles thereof under HS chapter 72 constitute $22.5 million. Similarly, under HS chapter 22, Bhutan has export potential of mineral water and alcohol worth $5.4 million annually. The identified products constitute a total worth of $116 million in exports to other countries, yet these are not exported to Bangladesh. Currently, Bangladesh imports the same products with an aggregate worth of $1,281 million from other countries rather than from Bhutan.

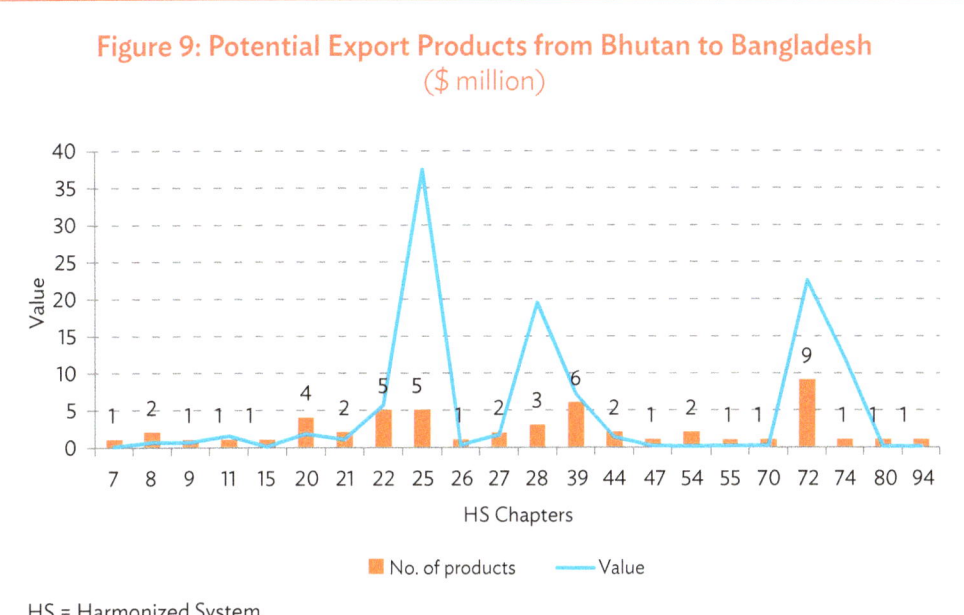

Figure 9: Potential Export Products from Bhutan to Bangladesh ($ million)

HS = Harmonized System.

Notes:
1. HS 7: Edible vegetables and certain roots and tubers.
2. HS 8: Edible fruit and nuts; peel of citrus fruit or melons.
3. HS 9: Coffee, tea, mate, and spices.
4. HS 11: Products of the milling industry; malt; starches; inulin; wheat gluten.
5. HS 15: Animal or vegetable fats and oils and their cleavage products; prepared edible fats; animal or vegetable waxes.
6. HS 20: Preparations of vegetables, fruit, nuts, or other parts of plants.
7. HS 21: Miscellaneous edible preparations.
8. HS 22: Beverages, spirits, and vinegar.
9. HS 25: Salt; sulfur; earths and stone; plastering materials, lime and cement.
10. HS 26: Ores, slag, and ash.
11. HS 27: Mineral fuels, mineral oils, and products of their distillation; bituminous substances; mineral waxes.
12. HS 28: Inorganic chemicals; organic or inorganic compounds of precious metals.
13. HS 39: Plastics and articles thereof.
14. HS 44: Wood and articles of wood; wood charcoal.
15. HS 47: Pulp of wood or of other fibrous cellulosic material; waste and scrap of paper or paperboard.
16. HS 54: Sewing thread of synthetic filaments, whether or not put up for retail sale.
17. HS 55: Synthetic staple fibers.
18. HS 70: Glass and glassware.
19. HS 72: Iron and steel.
20. HS 74: Copper and articles thereof.
21. HS 80: Tin and articles thereof.
22. HS 94: Furniture; bedding, mattresses.

Source: Government of Bhutan, Ministry of Finance, Department of Revenue and Customs. *Bhutan Trade Statistics 2016*. Thimphu.

Potential Export Products from Bhutan to India

The study identified a total of 1,811 potential products based on data for 2011–2015. Applying the filtering process, the following products were identified for export to India:

(i) filter 1 identified 740 products, reduced to 392 after removing duplicates;
(ii) filter 2 identified 164 products;
(iii) filter 3 identified 156 products;
(iv) filter 4 identified 117 products;
(v) filter 5 identified 13 products with an average export value from Bhutan to India of at least $24,000; and
(vi) filter 6 identified 13 products with an average import value into India from Bhutan of less than $24,000.

Figure 10 shows the 13 potential products for export from Bhutan to India, grouped by two-digit HS code. These 13 potential products are valued in total at $16 million. They are exported from Bhutan to other countries, but in lesser quantities to India. However, India's annual imports of the same products from other countries are recorded at $2,250 million, indicating a huge potential market for increased Bhutanese exports to India. Under HS code 25, Bhutan has the potential to export gypsum, cement, and boulders, while under HS chapter 08, there is potential to export apples and oranges.

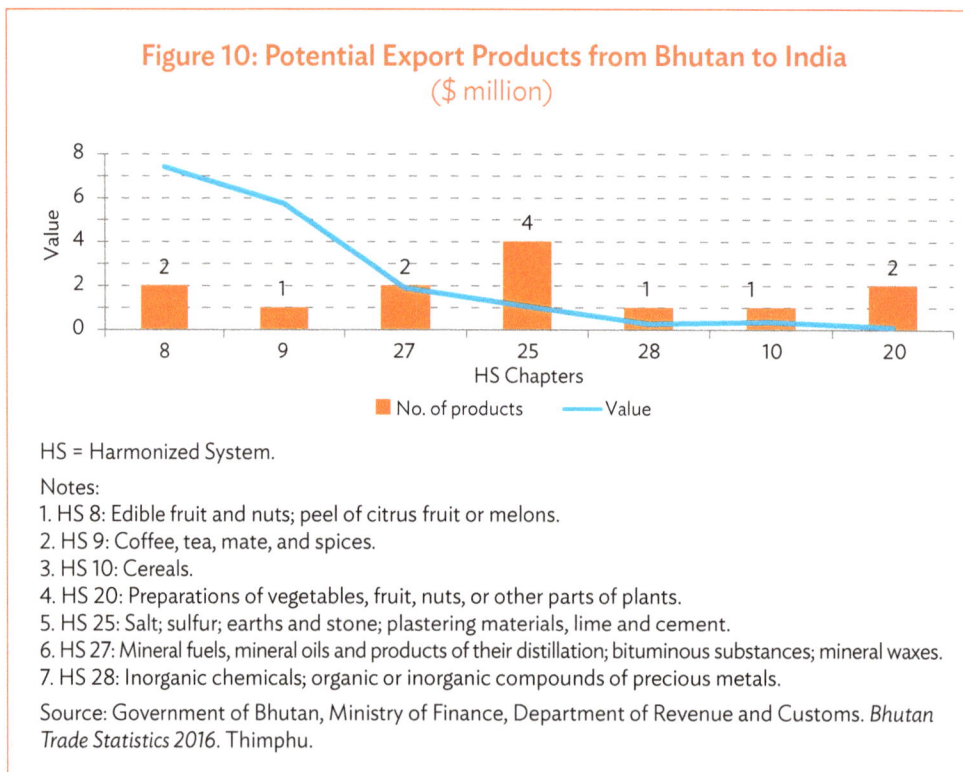

Figure 10: Potential Export Products from Bhutan to India
($ million)

HS = Harmonized System.
Notes:
1. HS 8: Edible fruit and nuts; peel of citrus fruit or melons.
2. HS 9: Coffee, tea, mate, and spices.
3. HS 10: Cereals.
4. HS 20: Preparations of vegetables, fruit, nuts, or other parts of plants.
5. HS 25: Salt; sulfur; earths and stone; plastering materials, lime and cement.
6. HS 27: Mineral fuels, mineral oils and products of their distillation; bituminous substances; mineral waxes.
7. HS 28: Inorganic chemicals; organic or inorganic compounds of precious metals.

Source: Government of Bhutan, Ministry of Finance, Department of Revenue and Customs. *Bhutan Trade Statistics 2016*. Thimphu.

Potential Export Products from Bhutan to Nepal

The study identified a total of 1,789 potential products based on data for 2011–2015. Applying the filtering process, the following products were identified for export to Nepal:

(i)   filter 1 identified 742 products, reduced to 392 after removing duplicates;
(ii) filter 2 identified 173 products;
(iii) filter 3 identified 172 products;
(iv) filter 4 identified 164 products;
(v)   filter 5 identified 101 products with an average export value from Bhutan to Nepal of at least $100,000; and
(vi) filter 6 identified 101 products with an average import value into Nepal from Bhutan of less than $100,000.

Figure 11 shows the 101 identified potential export products from Bhutan to Nepal grouped by 2-digit HS code, which constitute a potential total worth of $278 million. These products are exported to other countries, but either in negligible quantity or not at all to Nepal. On the other hand, Nepal imports the same products worth $645 million from other countries, but not from Bhutan. Under HS chapter 72, Bhutan has annual exports surpassing $152 million of mainly ferrosilicon, bars and rods of steel. This is followed by Bhutan's export competitiveness in Portland cement, dolomite, and calcium carbide under inorganic chemical compounds, under HS chapter 25. Copper and articles of copper constitute close to $2 million in exports annually.

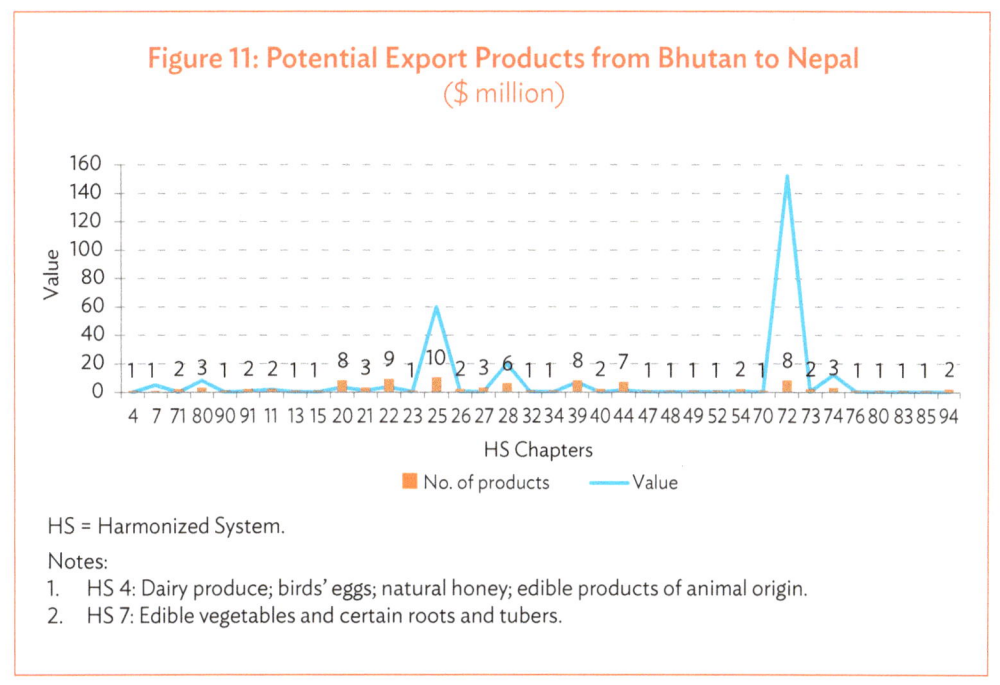

Figure 11: Potential Export Products from Bhutan to Nepal
($ million)

HS = Harmonized System.
Notes:
1. HS 4: Dairy produce; birds' eggs; natural honey; edible products of animal origin.
2. HS 7: Edible vegetables and certain roots and tubers.

continued on next page

Figure 11 continued

3. HS 11: Products of the milling industry; malt; starches; inulin; wheat gluten.
4. HS 13: Lac; gums, resins, and other vegetable saps and extracts.
5. HS 15: Animal or vegetable fats and oils and their cleavage products; prepared edible fats; animal or vegetable waxes.
6. HS 20: Preparations of vegetables, fruit, nuts, or other parts of plants.
7. HS 21: Miscellaneous edible preparations.
8. HS 22: Beverages, spirits, and vinegar.
9. HS 23: Residues and waste from the food industries; prepared animal fodder.
10. HS 25: Salt; sulfur; earths and stone; plastering materials, lime and cement.
11. HS 26: Ores, slag, and ash.
12. HS 27: Mineral fuels, mineral oils, and products of their distillation; bituminous substances; mineral waxes.
13. HS 28: Inorganic chemicals; organic or inorganic compounds of precious metals.
14. HS 32: Tanning or dyeing extracts; tannins and their derivatives; dyes, pigments, and other coloring matter; paints and varnishes; putty and other mastics; inks.
15. HS 34: Soap, organic surface-active agents, washing preparations.
16. HS 39: Plastics and articles thereof.
17. HS 40: Rubber and articles thereof.
18. HS 44: Wood and articles of wood; wood charcoal.
19. HS 47: Pulp of wood or of other fibrous cellulosic material; waste and scrap of paper or paperboard.
20. HS 48: Paper and paperboard; articles of paper pulp, of paper, or of paperboard.
21. HS 49: Printed books, newspapers, pictures, and other products of the printing industry; manuscripts, typescripts.
22. HS 52: Cotton.
23. HS 54: Sewing thread of synthetic filaments, whether or not put up for retail sale.
24. HS 70: Glass and glassware.
25. HS 71: Natural or cultured pearls, precious or semiprecious stones, precious metals, metals clad with precious metal, and articles thereof; imitation jewelry; coin.
26. HS 72: Iron and steel.
27. HS 73: Articles of iron or steel.
28. HS 74: Copper and articles thereof.
29. HS 76: Aluminum and articles thereof.
30. HS 80: Tin and articles thereof.
31. HS 83: Miscellaneous articles of base metal.
32. HS 85: Electrical machinery and equipment and parts thereof
33. HS 90: Optical, photographic, cinematographic, measuring, checking, precision, medical, or surgical instruments and apparatus.
34. HS 91: Clocks and watches and parts thereof.
35. HS 94: Furniture; bedding, mattresses

Source: Government of Bhutan, Ministry of Finance, Department of Revenue and Customs. *Bhutan Trade Statistics 2016.* Thimphu.

Chapter 4
Overview of Sanitary and Phytosanitary and Technical Barriers to Trade in Bhutan

Having identified potential export products from Bhutan to SASEC trading partners, chapter 4 examines SPS- and TBT-related legal frameworks, institutions, and infrastructure in Bhutan. The chapter outlines gaps comparing current national SPS legislation, local practices, and international best practices, corresponding to standards, institutions, infrastructure, and procedural issues and obstacles. The identification process is intended to help trading partners understand Bhutan's SPS and TBT measures, and to provide context for how Bhutan's potential export products may be impacted.

Several SASEC member countries are still working to build a robust basis for the proper implementation and enforcement of SPS measures, aligned with international best practice, as the standards and procedural requirements are demanding and require long-term planning and considerable resource allocation by national governments.

While Bhutan is not a member of the World Trade Organization and is therefore not bound under the Agreement on the Application of SPS Measures or the Agreement on TBT, it does aspire to an organic agricultural future cultivated within its pristine Himalayan environment.[17] As such, it has a heightened interest to protect its people, plants, and animals from transboundary disease, contaminants, and industrial pollution and damage.

The Sanitary and Phytosanitary Scenario

The Legal Structure

Bhutan's legal and regulatory SPS frameworks are relatively young, reflecting the short amount of time that Bhutan has actively sought to trade with diverse international markets. The following list details the legal documents that govern domestic food safety and quality.

Food Act of Bhutan 2005

The purpose of the Food Act of Bhutan is to protect human health and regulate and facilitate the import, export, and trade of food in Bhutan.[18] The act is guided by the National Food Quality and Safety Commission, and implemented through the Food Rules and

---

[17] World Trade Organization. Accessions. Bhutan.
[18] Government of Bhutan, Office of the Attorney General. 2005. *Food Act of Bhutan, 2005*. Thimphu.

Regulations of Bhutan 2017.[19] Chapter VI, section 39 of the act empowers BAFRA to carry out inspections on food establishments and to provide enforcement functions to ensure food safety and quality. Bhutan ensures food utilization in terms of hygiene and safety through a food inspectorate system. Under Chapter VIII of the act, BAFRA is sanctioned to enforce and ensure food safety and quality, and is granted certification responsibilities for both exports and imports. Crucially, Chapter II, section IX of the act vested the formation of the National Codex Committee. The committee is responsible for drafting national food standards as laid down under Chapter V, section 31 (d) and Chapter III, section 18 g (i) with reference to international and regional standards and practices. The Codex Contact Point, designated within BAFRA, serves as the secretariat for the committee, acting on its behalf in performing essential day-to-day tasks.

Biosafety Act of Bhutan 2015

The Biosafety Act of Bhutan prohibits import or transit of genetically modified organisms (GMOs) or living modified organisms into the country.[20] In addition, the act focuses on managing risks of adverse effects on biodiversity, the environment, and human and animal health. However, the act does not regulate (i) traditional and domestic methods of animal and plant breeding; (ii) traditional and domestic exchange and sale of local seeds, plants, and livestock; (iii) gene sequencing, tissue culture, and other similar methods, which do not involve the use of modern biotechnology; or (iv) products derived from GMOs for pharmaceuticals for human and/or veterinary use. The Biosafety Rules and Regulations 2018 facilitate effective implementation of the act.[21]

Plant Quarantine Act of Bhutan 1993

Chapter V of the Plant Quarantine Act prohibits the import of goods, plant products, and soil that are likely to pose threats to biodiversity.[22] It also issues regulations to prevent either the introduction or spread of plant pests. Chapter V of the act also empowers the quarantine inspector to quarantine any carrier, plant, plant product, good, or soil that is, or is likely to be, infested with a plant pest, and to order treatment in those cases. If a quarantine inspector deems that they cannot be effectively disinfested, or the contamination removed, the inspector may order (in writing) their destruction.

Livestock Act of Bhutan 2001

Chapter VII article 16.1 of the Livestock Act supports the Ministry of Agriculture and Forests to set standards pertaining to slaughtering facilities for livestock and poultry birds.[23] The Medicines Act of the Kingdom of Bhutan 2003 has repealed the functions that permit the Ministry of Agriculture and Forests (i) to set standards for veterinary drugs and (ii) to issue licenses to control importation, production, and distribution of veterinary drugs or

---

[19] Government of Bhutan, Ministry of Agriculture and Forests, BAFRA. 2017. *Food Rules and Regulations of Bhutan, 2017*. Thimphu.
[20] Government of Bhutan, Office of the Attorney General. 2015. *Biosafety Act of Bhutan 2015*. Thimphu.
[21] Government of Bhutan, Ministry of Agriculture and Forests, BAFRA. Biosafety Rules and Regulations 2018.
[22] Government of Bhutan, Office of the Attorney General. 1993. *Plant Quarantine Act of Bhutan, 1993*. Thimphu.
[23] Government of Bhutan, Office of the Attorney General. 2001. *Livestock Act of Bhutan, 2001*. Thimphu.

biological and therapeutic substances. This responsibility is now carried out by the Drug Regulatory Authority. All concerns regarding livestock inspection and certification are outlined in four sections under Chapter V of the act. Similarly, fresh meat hygiene and inspection are detailed under Chapter VII of the act.

Pesticides Act of Bhutan 2000

The Pesticides Act ensures only appropriate types of pesticides are introduced into Bhutan.[24] The act has stringent measures where an entity that desires to import pesticides must file an application to the minister of agriculture and forests. Imports of pesticides are regulated from the approved list of pesticides and governed by stringent regulations in terms of distribution and usage.

The following committees and boards have been established to oversee implementation of SPS-related legislation in Bhutan:

- (i) National Food Quality and Safety Commission,
- (ii) Management Board of BAFRA,
- (iii) National Pesticide Board,
- (iv) National Codex Committee,
- (v) Centenary Farmers Market Management Committee, and
- (vi) National Biosafety Board.

Salient SPS-related instruments and manuals in place include the following:[25]

- (i) Food Handling and Training Manual,
- (ii) Good Hygiene and Manufacturing Practices of Licensing Food Businesses,
- (iii) Food Safety Measures of Food Businesses,
- (iv) Training Manual of Meat Handlers,
- (v) Training Manual of Street Food Vendors,
- (vi) Food Safety and Investigation Manuals,
- (vii) Food Recall Guidance Manual,
- (viii) Bhutan Surveillance and Monitoring Program,
- (ix) In-country Livestock Biosecurity Guidelines,
- (x) Quarantine Station Operation Manual,
- (xi) Bhutan Animal Health Code for Import of Animals,
- (xii) online application system for processing and approval of permit or certificate for import or export of animals or plants and their products that facilitate importers and exporters, and
- (xiii) online application system for in-country movement of live animals.

These five acts consider environmental, human, animal, and plant health, and do not render trade as their sole or primary goal. Nonetheless, legal instruments of this type facilitate trade either through imports or exports. Bhutan is gradually improving expert services on

---

[24] Government of Bhutan, Office of the Attorney General. 2000. *Pesticides Act of Bhutan, 2000*. Thimphu.
[25] Government of Bhutan, Ministry of Agriculture and Forests. BAFRA.

import and export certification, rules of origin certification, value addition certification, food safety and quality certification, laboratory tests, and test result documentations that facilitate trade. However, there remains room for improvement.

The Institutional Framework

Bhutan Agriculture and Food Regulatory Authority

BAFRA governs the implementation of SPS measures in Bhutan. It was established in 2000 under the former Quality Control and Regulatory Services, with the minister of agriculture and forests as the chair of the management board. BAFRA has significant responsibilities, including ensuring food safety and quality, plant and animal biosecurity through quarantine measures, and biodiversity protection and pest management.

BAFRA is responsible for implementing the Plant Quarantine Act, Seeds Act of Bhutan 2000, Pesticides Act, Forest Nature and Conservation Act of Bhutan 2007, Food Act, and the Livestock Act. To enable holistic organic agriculture, BAFRA is also responsible for implementing the Biosafety Act of Bhutan 2015, carrying out inspection and certification of food and agricultural products (including organic produce) to ensure its quality and safety and also facilitate trade and increase market access. There are several rules to facilitate implementation, including the Plant Quarantine Rules and Regulations 2003 and 2018, Seed Rules and Regulations of Bhutan 2006, Food Rules and Regulations of Bhutan 2007, Livestock Rules and Regulations of Bhutan 2008, and the Biosecurity Policy of the Kingdom of Bhutan 2010.

BAFRA collaborates with key technical departments for implementation support of SPS measures, including the Department of Livestock and the Department of Agriculture (both under the Ministry of Agriculture and Forests), the Department of Public Health (under the Ministry of Health), and the Department of Revenue and Customs (under the Ministry of Finance).

BAFRA is the apex enforcement authority tasked with managing official entry and exit points for import and export inspection on regulatory and quarantine for livestock, plants, and food. It is also responsible for (i) the issuance of export certificates for agricultural, livestock, and food products; (ii) import control over livestock and plants and their products; and (iii) food safety. All SPS permits to import or export food and agricultural goods and products must be secured from BAFRA. Similarly, BAFRA issues the in-country permits that allow for the movement of plants and animals and their products within Bhutan.

Although Bhutan is only an observer member of the World Trade Organization, BAFRA serves as its national enquiry point for the implementation of the World Trade Organization Agreement on the Application of SPS Measures. In this capacity, it disseminates information to the public, exporters, and importers regarding product standards and quality parameters.

National Food Testing Laboratory

The National Food Testing Laboratory (NFTL), formerly called the National Quality Control Laboratory, was established in 2005 in Yusipang, Thimphu. Working in close cooperation with BAFRA, the NFTL provides testing facilities and generates reports for food microbiology, residues, contaminants, nutrition, and GMO detection to ensure the quality and safety of food and agricultural products. In practice, testing is limited to processed fruits and vegetable products; cereal and cereal products like biscuits, maize, grits, rice, and bread; tea, beverages, and drinking water; milk and dairy products; honey; oils and fats; and bakery products.[26] The NFTL carries out simple tests for the presence of soluble solids; acidity; moisture content; ash and acid insoluble ash; fat and protein content; pH levels; and the presence of heavy metals like lead, cadmium, and zinc. The NFTL has accredited 14 parameters based on the International Organization for Standardization (ISO)/International Electrotechnical Commission (IEC) 17025 standard, including microbiological and chemical disciplines. Other agencies oversee laboratories for seed products, and veterinary and animal feed.[27]

The NFTL is also mandated to monitor veterinary drug residues and food additives in foods of animal origin sold on the local market based on ISO/IEC 17025—these are general requirements for the competence of testing and calibration of laboratories. However, during its field visit to the NFTL, the study team did not observe the use of testing methods based on standard analytical methods, nor did it observe the adoption or use of published analytic methods or internationally recognized methods.

As of February 2018, the Food Safety and Security Authority of India (FSSAI) had initiated recognition of the NFTL for analysis of food samples under India's Food Safety and Standards Regulations 2011, requiring food import authorities in India to accept test analysis certificates issued by the NFTL.[28] The NFTL collaborates with the Mumbai Board of Radiation and Isotope Technology for specific test parameters of nonradioactive materials, although the high costs associated with such testing is a constraint.[29] The NFTL also works closely with the Export Inspection Council of India and with identified laboratories in Thailand on testing parameters that are beyond the scope of the NFTL.

Infrastructure Facilities

In addition to its headquarters in Thimphu, BAFRA has established offices in all 20 *dzongkhags* (administrative districts) and in nine *dungkhags* (subdistricts). Each has at least one BAFRA official and is responsible for implementing and enforcing SPS measures (Table 1).

---

[26] Government of Bhutan, Ministry of Agriculture and Forests, BAFRA. *National Food Testing Laboratory Progress Report, January–March 2016*. Thimphu.
[27] Government of Bhutan, Ministry of Agriculture and Forests, BAFRA. NFTL.
[28] Government of India, FSSAI. 2018. *File No. 12012/45/2017-QA*. New Delhi (6 February).
[29] NFTL program director, in conversation with the study team, October 2017.

Table 1: Sanitary and Phytosanitary-Related Infrastructure in Bhutan

Infrastructure Type	Number of Facilities	Location
BAFRA head office	1	Thimphu
BAFRA district offices	20	Established in all 20 dzongkhags[a]
BAFRA dungkhag (subdistrict) offices	9	Dagapela, Gedu, Gomtu, Gyelpoizhing, Jomotshagkha, Lamoizingkha, Panbang, Samdrupcholing, and Womrang
National Food Testing Laboratory	1	Yusipang, Thimphu
Plant and animal quarantine stations	6	Gelephu, Paro, Phuentsholing, Samdrup Jongkhar, and Samtse; Nganglam station soon to open

BAFRA = Bhutan Agriculture and Food Regulatory Authority

[a] A *dzongkhag* is an administrative district.

Source: Asian Development Bank consultant interviews with the Bhutan Agriculture and Food Regulatory Authority in 2017 and 2018.

Plant and animal quarantine stations have been built at six major entry points: Gelephu, Paro International Airport, Phuentsholing, Nganglam, Samdrup Jongkhar, and Samtse. There are five functional quarantine stations located in Gelephu, Paro International Airport, Phuentsholing, Samdrup Jongkhar, and Samtse, while one located in Nganglam is yet to be operationalized. The government has also constructed six small quarantine stations at border points to facilitate safe and efficient trade.

Plant and animal quarantine stations are present at Paro International Airport, where officials monitor the importation of ornamental plants, fresh fruits, vegetables, seeds, fresh meat, and pet animals. Basic test equipment facilities are available for identifying or screening suspected diseases or infections, but equipment for screening pests and diseases for plants or plant products is not yet adequate. Quarantine amnesty bins are available at the airport to raise awareness among the general public of BAFRA quarantine measures. There is no greenhouse facility for post-entry quarantine at Paro International Airport, but this is included in plans for future construction.

The NFTL in Yusipang houses the most modern and comprehensive testing equipment in Bhutan, including a gas chromatograph mass spectrometer; high-performance liquid chromatography; an atomic absorption spectrometer; and a real-time polymerase chain reaction machine used to detect residues of pesticides, antibiotics, drug residues, heavy metals, and mycotoxins or aflatoxins.

Export to and import from India is driven by market proximity and competitiveness, in addition to long-standing friendly bilateral relations. Under the trade and transit agreement between Bhutan and India (renewed on 20 November 2016), an additional five entry and exit points in India have been negotiated for trade: Dalu, Gasupara, Kulkuli, Loksan, and Nagakata. The agreement stipulates that "all exports and imports of Bhutan to and from countries other than India will be free from and not subject to customs duties and trade restrictions of the Government of the Republic of India," and lays out the procedures and documentation for such exports and imports (footnote 11, p. 2). Table 2 provides a complete list of all 21 entry and exit points and their descriptions.

Table 2: Trade Entry and Exit Points in India for Import to and Export from Bhutan

Series No.	Description	Entry-Exit Points
1	Road route	Chamurchi, Changrabandh, Chennai, Darranga, Dawki, Hathisar (Gelephu), Jaigaon, Panitanki, Phulbari, Ulta Pani
2	Road and rail route	Raxaul
3	Road route on a seasonal basis	Kulkuli, Loksan, Nagarkata
4	Road route for export and import of Bhutanese cargo from and to Bangladesh	Dalu
5	Road route for export of Bhutanese cargo to Bangladesh	Gasupara
6	Air route	New Delhi
7	Air and sea route	Kolkata
8	Sea route	Haldia
9	Sea and air route	Mumbai
10	Riverine route[a]	Dhubri

[a] To date, this route has not been used, although inland water transport from the Brahmaputra River has been notified by the Government of India.

Source: Government of Bhutan and Government of India. 2016. *Agreement on Trade, Commerce and Transit between the Royal Government of Bhutan and the Government of the Republic of India*. Thimphu.

As is the case with India, several trade routes are agreed between Bhutan and Bangladesh, as outlined in the Protocol to the Agreement on Trade between the Royal Government of Bhutan, and the Government of the People's Republic of Bangladesh signed on 6 December 2014 (Table 3).[30]

Sections 4.1.4–4.1.6 detail the most pressing gaps identified in SPS-related legislation and rules and regulations, institutional structures, and infrastructure. These were identified based on findings from surveys and interviews with relevant stakeholders, together with analysis of current legislation and procedures.

---

[30] Government of Bhutan and Government of Bangladesh. 2014. Protocol to the Agreement on Trade between the Royal Government of Bhutan and the Government of the People's Republic of Bangladesh. Dhaka.

Table 3: Identified Trade Routes for Bhutan and Bangladesh

Series No.	Bhutan Trade Routes	Bangladesh Trade Routes
1	Samdrup Jongkhar	Moghalhat
2	Gelephu	Noonkhawa
3	Sarpang	Nakugaon
4	Phuentsholing	Haluaghat
5	Samtse	Banglabandha
6	Paro International Airport	Burimari
7	--	Hazrat Shajalal International Airport (Dhaka)
8	--	Shah Amanat International Airport (Chittagong)
9	--	Tamabil

Source: Government of Bhutan and Government of Bangladesh. 2014. *Protocol to the Agreement on Trade between the Royal Government of Bhutan and the Government of the People's Republic of Bangladesh*. Dhaka.

Gaps in Legislation

Overlapping authority. Chapter III section 18g(i) of the Food Act draws up standards, while Chapter II section IV of the Bhutan Standards Act 2010 stipulates the same functions to develop national standards and facilitate their implementation. This results in two different acts empowering two different institutions with the same functions of standard setting.

Potential conflicts of interest. Challenges to draft standards in several consumer food items remain high, and members of technical committees take on the task of drafting standards as an added responsibility. The Food Act stipulates, however, that BAFRA take on responsibilities of the food inspectorate system, laboratory testing, quarantine measures, and certification. Simultaneous engagement in drafting standards, testing, and providing certification could result in a conflict of interest arising from a single institution certifying its own test results.

As noted, BAFRA falls under the Ministry of Agriculture and Forests. However, this can lead to complexities enforcing SPS measures because agencies such as the Department of Livestock, the Department of Forests and Park Services, and the Department of Agriculture are housed under the same ministry. The risk of conflicts of interest creates the potential for dilution of BAFRA functions.

Limited food safety surveillance. There are no established standard operating procedures relating to the lack of sample testing on a regular basis for consumable items. Food safety tests are carried out only when there is a situation that poses a threat to public health. For example, laboratory tests on chilies from Falakata, West Bengal state, India showed pesticide residue beyond safe limits, forcing the Government of Bhutan to enforce a ban on imports from this production area.[31] Similar issues arise with imported seaweed and suspected detection of inorganic arsenic and cadmium residue beyond maximum residue limits.[32] Ad hoc testing is carried out only on a reactionary basis when a public health safety alarm surfaces. More robust standard operating procedures would counter this gap in implementation.

Limited testing and certification resources to support exports. Recognition of BAFRA certification can be delayed for certain products of exports such as ultra-high temperature milk and fruit juices.[33] Importers require test results from recognized institutions such as the FSSAI. Similarly, for export of cardamom to India, SPS certification issued by BAFRA is not acknowledged without the need for detailed additional information. Authorities in India often require a "fit for human consumption" certificate issued by reputed institutes in India. The closest of these is in Kolkata, which can lead to delays of up to 10 days and extra costs. Similar problems exist for all fruit products exported to Bangladesh, where importers require formalin-free test results and nonradioactive test results. With no testing facilities in Bhutan, samples are sent to India (Mumbai) and Thailand, incurring long delays and extra cost.

Institutional Gaps

Laboratory facilities. The NFTL has constructed each of its laboratory components in different locations, which impedes the effective sharing of resources including equipment, water, and heating. For example, the microbiology, biotechnology, contaminants, and nutritional laboratories are each housed in different buildings, requiring installation of independent heating and cooling facilities for each. The layout also does not permit common sample testing. The NFTL also has limited technical capacity and equipment. As a result, its tests only accommodate basic parameters of moisture content and the presence of soluble materials. Because of the lack of well-equipped technical laboratory facilities, most samples requiring sophisticated testing are sent to India or Thailand. For example, the Mumbai Board of Radiation and Isotope Technology of the Department of Atomic Energy in India helps conduct radioactive substance test on agricultural products for export to Bangladesh. Similarly, collaboration with the Government of India's Export Inspection Council is required for testing and certifying high-risk food commodities for import into Bhutan. In addition to added costs, the need to outsource laboratory functions creates delays, while outsourcing these functions to other countries leads to missed opportunities to build capacity within Bhutan.

Laboratory accreditation. Despite resource constraints, the NFTL has made all relevant efforts to follow best practices in terms of testing protocols and standard operating procedures, and has secured ISO/IEC 17025 certification. However, this particular ISO certification only covers standard general requirements and competence of testing and calibration laboratories. Furthermore, the NFTL's international accreditation is contingent on the continued employment of technical and skilled human resources, which will require recurrent budgetary commitment.

---

[31] T. Lamsang. 2016. BAFRA bans import of all types of chillies due to pesticides. *The Bhutanese*. 23 July.
[32] Government of Bhutan, Ministry of Agriculture and Forests. 2016. *Notification BAFRA/MoAF/5-47/170*. Thimphu.
[33] Representatives of Zimdra Foods Limited, in conversation with the author, July 2017.

Limited human resources. There are few qualified nationals to manage capacity building efforts needed to ensure proper biosecurity and to improve food safety both from imports and domestic production—both of which are essential to national well-being (Table 4). Furthermore, the vast mandate of responsibilities under the existing organizational structure for the Quality Control and Quarantine Division and the Analytical and Certification Division overburdens BAFRA management. Personnel are spread across responsibilities of food inspection, laboratory testing, surveillance and compliance, standard setting, plant and animal biosecurity, biosafety, import inspection, and export certification while covering items of food, feed, plant, agriproducts, animals, livestock products, and non-wood forest products.

Overall, BAFRA lacks essential resources to meet institutional mandates and ensure public health. Key resource constraints include lack of skilled and experienced human resources, an inadequate budget, and limited transport resources.

Export constraints into Bangladesh. Certification demands from Bangladesh are laborious, with independent requirements for each test parameter: all imports to Bangladesh should produce 4–5 separate certificate sheets, rather than acknowledging all tests in a single sheet. The Government of Bangladesh requires test certificates confirming the absence of formalin and radioactive materials in apples and mandarins as part of national legislative requirements, in addition to the phytosanitary certificate issued by BAFRA.

Gaps in Infrastructure

Bhutan lacks adequate laboratories and personnel to carry out the required tests both to certify exports and monitor imports. Most tests are outsourced by sending samples to India and Thailand, incurring high costs and delays. The NFTL's capacity to test and ensure SPS compliance is limited to basic testing parameters such as soluble solids; acidity; moisture content; ash and acid-insoluble ash; fat and protein content; and pH levels and the presence of heavy metals like lead, cadmium, and zinc. Tests requiring sophisticated equipment or techniques are sent to other countries.

Other specific concerns include the following:

(i) insufficient and inadequate facilities for quality testing and certification;
(ii) inadequate capacity to comply with risk assessment and laboratory testing measures;
(iii) lack of analytical capacity in the NFTL to analyze chemical residues, pesticide residues, mycotoxins, heavy metals, veterinary drug residues, and microbiological risk in food items;
(iv) high compliance cost for exporting citrus and apples owing to quality requirements in Bangladesh and the need to outsource testing to India and Thailand; and
(v) mismatch between resources allocated to BAFRA and the services it needs to provide.

Table 4 indicates that satellite laboratory stations are managed by a single laboratory technician and are poorly equipped with testing facilities. For example, the Phuentsholing satellite laboratory is almost nonfunctional, and the BAFRA office building is shared with the Road Safety and Transport Authority. This increases the level of people traffic, which risks cross-contamination, especially during specimen sample testing. A severe lack of qualified and competent staff and equipment is another key challenge that remains to be addressed.

Furthermore, laboratory testing facilities at the NFTL are outdated and incur sustained high costs because of inadequate equipment maintenance contracts with local suppliers (Table 9). In some cases, NFTL equipment was procured from suppliers outside of South Asia. This makes it difficult to request and receive training on equipment and software usage, and has led to limited availability of spare parts. For example, the gas chromatograph mass spectrometer supplied by the Shimadzu brand has become obsolete, and since the supplier is not nearby, it has proven difficult to replace parts and receive support for software calibration and training for technicians at the national laboratory in Yusipang. It will be necessary to replace obsolete high-precision equipment, including the gas chromatograph mass spectrometer and other instruments, to cope with demand.[34]

The lack of abattoirs in Bhutan compromises the safety and quality of beef imported from India, leaving it to be done informally as there are no facilities in India that process beef. Because of the lack of proper abattoir facilities in the country, the transportation of imported fresh meat to major markets is done in regular vehicles customized to meet basic transportation requirements in the absence of freezer amenities. Storage and sales counters are rudimentary.

Table 4: Infrastructure and Human Resource of Laboratory Facilities

Infrastructure Type	Year Built	No. of Human Resources Employed	Testing Parameters	Location	Commodities Tested	Constraints
National Food Testing Laboratory	2005	14	Microbiology, residue, contaminants, GMOs, and nutrition[a]	Yusipang	Various products[b]	Lack of competent human resources and modern equipment
Satellite laboratory at Samtse	2014	1 Lab technician	Basic tests on quarantine samples and on-site food safety tests	Quarantine station	Quarantine samples and food samples	Laboratory space is small

continued on next page

---

[34] Program director, NFTL, Yusipang, in conversation with the author, June 2017.

Table 4 continued

Infrastructure Type	Year Built	No. of Human Resources Employed	Testing Parameters	Location	Commodities Tested	Constraints
Satellite laboratory at Phuentsholing	2014	1 Lab technician	Basic tests on quarantine samples and on-site food safety tests	Quarantine station	Quarantine samples and food samples	Lab housed in RSTA building
Satellite laboratory at Gelephu	2014	1 Lab technician	Basic tests on quarantine samples and on-site food safety tests	Quarantine station	Quarantine samples and food samples	Technician not adequately trained
Satellite laboratory at Samdrup Jongkhar	2014	1 Lab technician	Basic tests on quarantine samples and on-site food safety tests	Quarantine station	Quarantine samples and food samples	Technician not adequately trained
Satellite laboratory at Paro	2014	1 Lab technician	Basic tests on quarantine samples and on-site food safety tests	Quarantine station	Quarantine samples and food samples	Technician not adequately trained

GMO = genetically modified organism, RSTA = Road Safety and Transport Authority.

[a] A list of accredited test parameters can be found here: Government of Bhutan, Ministry of Agriculture and Forests, Bhutan Agriculture and Food Regulatory Authority. Scope of Accreditation.

[b] An exhaustive list of these products can found here: Government of Bhutan, Ministry of Agriculture and Forests, Bhutan Agriculture and Food Regulatory Authority. Scope of Accreditation.

Source: Asian Development Bank consultant, based on field visits, interviews, and desk research.

Technical Barriers to Trade Scenario

TBT issues fall under the mandate of various agencies, but the Bhutan Standards Bureau (BSB) is the lead organization tasked with overseeing compliance and certification in line with industry standards and requirements.

The Legal Structure

Bhutan Standards Act 2010

The Bhutan Standards Act governs TBT measures in Bhutan. It identifies which domestic entities will oversee product certification, and provides guidance on establishing associated schemes. The act mandates that the BSB implement a product certification scheme aligned with the requirements of ISO/IEC 17065:2012.[35] The BSB has accordingly implemented a product certification scheme, under BSB Regulation 2012. The scheme seeks to determine conformity of products to Bhutanese standards through product sampling, initial testing, and assessment of factory quality management systems. It covers domestically

---

[35] ISO/IEC 17065:2012 specifies the requirements for bodies certifying products, process, and services.

manufactured products within the framework of the Bhutan Standards Act and ISO/IEC 17065:2012.

Chapter II section IV of the Bhutan Standards Act mandates that the BSB develop national standards and facilitate their implementation. The act empowers the BSB to operate metrological referral and calibration laboratories. Other BSB functions include establishing and operating product testing infrastructure materials and calibrating equipment. The BSB also oversees the implementation of regional and international trade agreements related to standards and TBTs.

As Bhutan increasingly engages with international markets, the BSB has recognized the need to demonstrate equivalency with other countries' certification schemes, and to secure recognition of the BSB certification scheme by its trade partners, especially SAARC countries. The BSB is therefore working to achieve international accreditation for its product certification. The BSB charges fees for product certification in line with the national fee structure under its Product Brand Approval Scheme 2010, with associated revenue going to the government.

The Institutional Framework

The BSB was established as an autonomous organization in 2010 after the enactment of the Bhutan Standards Act on 7 July 2010. Its institutional mandate is to foster and promote standards and standardization activities as a means of (i) advancing the national economy; (ii) benefiting the health, safety, and welfare of the public; (iii) assisting and protecting consumers; (iv) protecting the natural environment; (v) promoting industrial efficiency and development, and (vi) facilitating domestic and international trade. The BSB holds responsibility in the core areas of standards, metrology, testing, and certification. It also provides supports to organizations seeking accreditation in relevant fields.

The BSB has established four technical divisions: (i) Standardization Division, (ii) Certification Division, (iii) Metrology and Laboratory Services Division, and (iv) International Relations Division.

The BSB is responsible for convening technical committees of experts to draft specific standards as they relate to different industries, products, and processes. Working closely with the technical committees, the BSB prepares policies on standardization and conformity assessment to promote high-quality goods and international competitiveness. The BSB has established technical committees with representatives from government agencies and the private sector, and through them, has started setting standards and issuing certification. The BSB's initial focus has been on preparing norms and regulations for the construction industry, and the BSB had already established the following 10 technical committees by 2017:

(i) Civil Engineering Technical Committee,
(ii) Food and Agriculture Technical Committee,
(iii) Electrical and Electronics Technical Committee,
(iv) Basic and Management Systems Technical Committee,

(v) Pharmaceuticals and Traditional Medicines Technical Committee,
(vi) Textiles Technical Committee,
(vii) Wood and Timber Products Technical Committee,
(viii) Mechanical Engineering Technical Committee,
(ix) Graphical Symbol Technical Committee, and
(x) Sustainable Environment Technical Committee.

In total, the BSB has drafted 164 national standards, including in the areas of (i) civil and mechanical engineering, (ii) food and agriculture, (iii) electrical and electronics, (iv) basic and management systems, (v) pharmaceuticals and traditional medicines, (vi) textiles, (vii) timber and wood products, and (viii) graphical symbols.[36] As the BSB gains knowledge and capacity, it plans to expand coverage to other areas such as public health and safety, and environmental protection. During the seventh BSB board meeting held in April 2017, Bhutan adopted a list of 21 national standards in the areas of road safety, mechanical engineering, electronic and electric engineering, wood and timber products, and civil engineering.

The BSB's certification body (ISO/IEC 17065) and metrology laboratory (mass and length) have been accredited to ISO/IEC 17025. Certification for products in three scopes of bitumen emulsion, thermo-mechanical treatment reinforcement bars, and cement are based on ISO/IEC 17065:2015. The metrology laboratory is accredited for two scopes: mass and length under ISO/IEC 17025:2005. The BSB has also signed a memorandum of understanding with the Bangladesh Standards and Testing Institution (BSTI) to foster cooperation in standardization, testing, and calibration.[37]

The BSB is the national focal point that facilitates accreditation of Bhutanese organizations. It is in the process of developing standards, metrology, testing, and quality infrastructure to support the limited range of products that Bhutan manufactures for domestic consumption and export. However, as the economy continues to grow and manufacturing activities become more diverse, there will be a growing need to develop further capacity and expand national testing and certification capability. This should involve internationally recognized standards, accredited laboratories, and certification institutions.[38] In the future, standard-setting bodies should be independent and separate from certification bodies, and all functions (including metrology, laboratory testing, and certification) should be independent from each other.

The BSB also serves as the nodal agency that represents Bhutan in the ISO/IEC, South Asian Regional Standards Organization (SARSO), Asia Pacific Laboratory Accreditation Cooperation, which was established in 2019 by the amalgamation of the Asia Pacific Laboratory Accreditation Cooperation and the Pacific Accreditation Cooperation. It is also the national enquiry point for World Trade Organization TBT matters.

---

[36] Chief engineer, Standardization Division, BSB, in conversation with the author, July 2017.
[37] Chief engineer, Certification Division, BSB, in conversation with the author, July 2017. Government of Bhutan, BSB. International Relations Division.
[38] Director general, BSB, in conversation with the author, July 2017.

Infrastructure Facilities

The Bhutan Standards Act recognizes that quality infrastructure is essential to the success of economic development and public safety. It indicates that quality infrastructure is vital to enhancing the competitiveness of Bhutan's local industries, promoting fair and efficient trade, and protecting the health and safety of consumers and the environment. The BSB has two central laboratories—the National Metrology Laboratory (NML), and the Product Testing Laboratory—both located within the BSB office complex in Thimphu. The NML offers calibration services for length, mass, volume, temperature, and pressure. The NML's calibration services include weights and electronic balances, steel scales and measuring tapes, calibration on volumetric measures, calibration on liquid in glass thermometers, and calibration on pressure gauges. The NML has been accredited by the National Accreditation Board for Testing and Calibration Laboratory of India for mass and length.[39] The NML also conducts tests for soil, stone aggregates, bitumen, steel, cement, building materials, coarse and fine materials, steel and steel components, and road grade (each with corresponding test fees).[40]

Gaps in Legislation

There remains a lack of clarity in understanding roles and mandates stipulated in the Bhutan Standards Act and those of the Food Act with particular reference to standard setting. Bhutan's national industry standards are still a work in progress, with only some standards drafted in the areas of (i) roads, (ii) mechanical engineering, (iii) electronics and electrical engineering, (iv) food and agriculture, (v) civil and mechanical engineering, (vi) textiles, and (vii) timber and wood products.

Institutional Gaps

Multiple standards. In addition to the BSB's 164 draft standards and 21 approved standards, Bhutan has close to 500 other standards that have been established by multiple domestic agencies. These 500 standards are in various stages of use or acceptance across a range of industries. There is limited national coordination among associated agencies with respect to standard setting, use, and implementation, which can create confusion during conformity assessments.

Barriers to enforcement. Although standards are being drafted with reference to ISO, IEC, and other regional standards, enforcement remains a challenge. In particular, there are no distinct mandates that clearly state which institution (such as the BSB, Office of Consumer Protection, or DRC) is responsible for safeguarding consumers of these products. For example, several products—including electrical wires, switches, and electrical bulbs—have flooded the Bhutanese market during the construction boom that began in 2016. Lack of local monitoring and enforcement of standards leaves consumers unable to distinguish the real product from imitations. Similar issues exist with imported building materials such as red bricks, plywood, and corrugated galvanized iron sheets.

---

[39] Deputy executive engineer, Metrology Division, BSB, in conversation with the author, July 2017.
[40] Government of Bhutan, BSB. BSB.

Good practices applied in select industries. Positive examples of adequate consumer protection do exist in Bhutan. For example, pharmaceutical imports are well regulated by the Drug Regulatory Authority, which screens imports and conducts surprise inspections to discourage illegal activity and to help ensure only permissible drugs are allowed into the country. Appropriate controls under the Drug Regulatory Authority were implemented as a result of previously weak surveillance, which had allowed substandard products to seep into Bhutan, despite the prevalence of authorized domestic wholesalers who are legally obliged to sell genuine quality products that are traceable to ensure quality.

Limited institutional capacity. The BSB lacks skilled personnel and capacity to execute its mandate as a standard-setting organization and service provider. For example, the Government of Bhutan has not furnished the BSB with sufficient professionals with mechanical engineering training. Likewise, there is a need for food chemists, bioscience graduates, and SPS and TBT experts to support food and agriculture standards and calibration. However, these skilled workers are either not available or in short supply. The lack of human resources for product certification stems from a lack of trained personnel domestically in the fields of electrical, mechanical, and chemical engineering. The BSB is making efforts to fulfill its institutional mandates with ad hoc training support delivered through international organizations.

Gaps in Infrastructure

As in the case of SPS-related infrastructure, availability of TBT-related laboratories and equipment remains limited in Bhutan, and testing facilities do not yet have international accreditation. The NML and Product Testing Laboratory are located in the same building, which leads to significant challenges in performing precise metrology functions. For instance, vibrations caused by product testing are felt throughout the building and prevent precision measurement.

Chapter 5
Standards, Regulations, and Procedural Obstacles in the SASEC Countries That Impede Bhutan Import and Export Trade

The national diagnostic study identified standards, regulations, and procedural obstacles that affect Bhutan's potential exports to Bangladesh, India, and Nepal based on (i) the online International Trade Center Trade Map database, (ii) available secondary research data, and (iii) collaborative consultation with SASEC experts responsible for corresponding national SPS and TBT diagnostic studies. Appendix 3 presents identified standards, regulations, and procedural obstacles on Bhutan's potential exports with Bangladesh, India, and Nepal. The tabular information highlights the ongoing SPS and TBT measures applied by both the importing countries (Bangladesh, India, and Nepal) and exporting country (Bhutan), including details corresponding to HS codes and implementing agencies.

Impediments while Exporting to Bangladesh

Standards and Regulations

Portland cement, gypsum, iron, calcium carbide, cement clinkers, and mineral water are subject to import certification from BSTI (Table 5). Imports of aerated mineral water are subject to B83 certification, requiring the submission of a certificate from BSTI to the customs authority. Ferroalloys have to undergo B7 product quality or performance requirement and C1 pre-shipment inspection, with only prime qualities allowed in the country.

Overall, all goods are subject to the Import Policy, 2012–2015 and governed by the Ministry of Commerce. Products including undenatured ethyl alcohol (HS code 220710), beer from malt (HS code 220300), waste and scraps of iron and tin (HS code 720430 and 800200), and whiskies (HS code 220830) all fall under the BSTI prohibition list applying G332 (importers' own foreign exchange), B19 (prohibitions or restrictions of imports for objectives set out in the TBT agreement) with only recognized bona fide user industrial units allowed to import iron and steel waste and scrap, and E329 (prohibition of imports for non-economic reasons).

For wheat or meslin flour (HS code 110100) and juice of fruit and vegetables (HS code 200989), the following standards and regulations apply: A22 (restricted use of certain substances in foods and feeds and their contact materials); A31 and A33 (labeling and packaging); and A82 (testing requirement), including a radioactivity level test. Further, these products require A83 certification of radioactivity levels and certification that the food is fit for human consumption, and submission of BSTI certification to the customs authority indicating the goods conform to Bangladesh Standards (BDS) 513:2002.

Table 5: Impediments while Exporting to Bangladesh

Products	Standards
Portland cement, gypsum, iron bars and rods, calcium carbide, cement clinkers and aerated mineral	– Require submission of an import certificate from BSTI to the customs authority – B83 certification requirements
Undenatured ethyl alcohol, beer from malt, waste and scrap of iron and tin, and whiskies	– Prohibition list set out in the TBT agreement
For wheat or meslin flour and juice of fruit and vegetables	– Restricted use of certain substances in foods and feeds and their contact materials – Standards and regulations of A22, A31, and A33 labeling and packaging, and A82 testing requirement, including radioactivity levels test – Fit for human consumption as well as certification from BSTI to the customs authority – Import Policy, 2012–2015
All kinds of fruits	– Requires third-country testing stating that fruits are free from formalin preservatives (e.g., oranges require spot-testing on border crossings into Bangladesh)

BSTI = Bangladesh Standards and Testing Institution, TBT = technical barrier to trade.
Source: Asian Development Bank consultant, based on interviews and desk research.

Other exports not accurately reflected in the list of potential exports (Appendix 2) include limestone powder (under HS code 2521). Limestone powder in particular has a duty-free classification but has been inaccurately classified by Bangladeshi importers under HS code 2417, which carries a 60% duty. This discrepancy has led to significant revenue losses for Bhutan from the temporary halt in exports while the two governments have addressed the issue. Similarly, Bangladeshi importers categorized calcium carbonate under HS code 2517 when it should have been under HS code 283650, leading to temporary closure of manufacturing plants. Some exporters expressed concerns on bilateral agreements, indicating that the memorandum of understanding between the BSB and BSTI was close to being breached.

Likewise, in 2017 Bangladesh required excessive radiological certificates for imported milk and milk products; edible oils; and other food items, including poultry and animal feed products and fruits. Potatoes required a health certificate indicating that the product was fit for human consumption and certificates of analysis were required for other food items. As a result, the standard phytosanitary certificate issued by BAFRA had to be accompanied by a (i) radiation-free certificate, (ii) a fit for human consumption certificate, and (iii) a formalin test certificate.

Onerous testing requirements and limited communication between officials. Historically, all fruits exported from Bhutan to Bangladesh required third-country testing and certification stating the product was free from formalin preservatives. However, formalin is not used in Bhutan. As such, fruit exporters were required to send samples from the border to accredited laboratories in India and wait for results prior to export, creating unnecessary delays that threatened the quality of perishable goods. Officials from the Bhutan Exporters Association noted that Bangladeshi authorities have since recognized the redundancy of formalin tests on Bhutanese fruits (paired with the limited infrastructure and technical capacity at the Bhutan–Bangladesh border-crossing points) and have waived formalin test requirements for Bhutanese fruits through policy amendments. However, in practice, border agents in Bangladesh have not been notified of the policy change and still require test results from accredited entities in India. The associated delays create a barrier to trade, as they cause unnecessary burdens for importers and exporters, and can degrade the quality of fruit exports.

Procedural

Banking inefficiencies. Delays caused by inefficient bank processes are a major barrier to bilateral trade. One of the main hurdles is slow processing of letters of credit. Banks in Bangladesh and Bhutan have lengthy and cumbersome documentation requirements for approving fund transfers. Exporters indicated that there are unnecessary delays before funds are credited by the Bangladeshi importer. A cardamom exporter stated that letter of credit clearance takes about a month, locking up cash and limiting business during the export season, as banking processes and terminology that is inconsistent with that of letter of credit terms and conditions cause confusion and delays.

Traffic congestion. Transborder shipments are also affected by limited infrastructure, heavy traffic congestion, and inefficient documentation requirements. For example, consignments entering Bangladesh need to clear border formalities at Burimari or Changrabandha. Interviews with exporters indicated that there were delays caused by traffic congestion, with both Indian and Bhutanese trucks using the same clearance checkpoints, overburdening available infrastructure. Since Indian trucks tend to carry larger consignments and are subject to different trade rules, the sentiment of many traders is that they should pass through different gates or border crossings to reduce congestion affecting non-Indian traders. Bhutanese exporters reported that during 2015–2016, trucks carrying mineral products were stranded for 6–7 days waiting in line on the road, incurring significant additional expenses from daily parking rentals, food, and other essentials. For some exporters, these additional costs are applied to more than 100 trucks every day.

Lack of information and communication technology. Limited information and communication facilities and cumbersome documentation requirements for export clearance result in high transaction costs. Although a national single window system is under development and a basic online application system exists for importers and exporters, there is no comprehensive information and communication technology system to facilitate documentation, which causes delays and inefficiency for traders and border officials alike. Documentation is inputted manually, and there are few customer windows to handle increasing trade volumes.

Service providers are also limited by a shortage or lack of border agency officials at the checkpoints. For example, in Burimari, the border crossing point closes every Friday, stranding consignments on the road for the weekend. Inadequate infrastructure at most border clearance points is a hindrance to trade, and infrastructure gaps are becoming more pronounced as new routes open.

Impediments while Exporting to India

Standards and Regulations

Any exported Bhutanese food article must be sent to laboratories authorized by the Food Safety and Security Authority of India (FSSAI). However, India does not acknowledge test certificates from BAFRA for processed food items, and instead requires test certificates from the FSSAI. Further regulations (and associated delays) exist for particular products. For example, ultra-high temperature milk requires quarantine testing of packaged milk to be done in India, and since the nearest test institute is in Kolkata, it takes close to 10 days to complete the laboratory results (Table 6). Orange, apple, and all other fruit juice exports to India require country-of-export certification and must be packed to facilitate inspection and sample collection. Exports to India must adhere to FSSAI's Food Safety and Standards (Food Product Standards and Food Additives) Amendment Regulations, 2016 and General Grading and Marking Rules 1998. Similarly, cardamom and pepper must be certified by laboratories in Kolkata to satisfy food safety requirements by customs authorities in India, prior to export.

BAFRA does not have mutual recognition agreements for certification with its counterparts in India. Lack of mutual recognition and equivalence of export inspection and certification systems requires BAFRA to have tests done either in India or in third-party countries such as Thailand. This causes delays and loss of business opportunities.

Table 6: Impediments while Exporting to India

Products	Standards
Orange, apple, and all other fruit juices	Must be packed to facilitate inspection and collection of samples, and requires country-of-export certification. Exports to India must adhere to the Food Safety and Standards (Food Product Standards and Food Additives) Amendment Regulations, 2016and General Grading and Marking Rules 1998.
Cardamom	Must satisfy food safety certification from reputed institutions in Kolkata.
Ultra-high temperature milk	BAFRA certification is not recognized by Indian importing partners and certification is a requirement at the checkpoints. Processed food items and ultra-high temperature milk require quarantine testing done in India. The nearest laboratory is in Kolkata and takes close to 10 days to get results.

BAFRA = Bhutan Agriculture and Food Regulatory Authority.
Source: Asian Development Bank consultant, based on interviews and desk research.

Changes in India's tax structure in 2017 made it a less competitive market for exports from Bhutan. In particular, India's introduction of a goods and services tax (GST) levies taxes on all imports under different tax slabs, compared to no or few taxes in the past. Under India's previous indirect tax regime, Bhutanese products exported to India were exempt from all taxes and duties, including countervailing duty, special additional duty, and customs duty. Goods imported into India are subject to a combination of both central government GST and state government GST, called integrated GST. With all exports to India now subject to integrated GST that must be paid to customs authorities at the Jaigaon border crossing point by Indian importers, these importers are looking to source alternatives from India, that are exempt from integrated GST. This change in the tax regime rendered some Bhutanese manufacturers uncompetitive against Indian manufacturers: for example, in 2017, integrated GST increased to 28% on cement, furniture, and particle board; and 18% on plastic materials and steel, rods, bars, ferrosilicon, and calcium carbide rose.

Procedural

Border-crossing facilities require upgrades, particularly in customs and transport formalities. Bhutan's industrial activities are concentrated in the south of the country, where the major industrial estates and cross-border facilities are located. Most freight transport occurs by road, and about 85% of imported goods pass into India through the border-crossing point near Phuentsholing in southwestern Bhutan. However, the existing border infrastructure cannot accommodate increasing traffic flow. Costly cargo movement between industrial centers and across borders curtails the country's trade and industrial potential.

Transportation of consignments from Bhutan to India is typically commissioned by Indian trucks and required to cross through several customs checkpoints. This entails delays and costs in the form of informal payments required to expedite road journeys.

Impediments while Exporting to Nepal

Standards and Regulations

Products including ferrosilicon and ferromanganese are subject to nontariff measures such as B1 prohibitions or restrictions on imports for objectives set out in the TBT agreement, B7 product quality or performance requirement, and B83 certification requirement (Table 7). Similarly, Portland cement, dolomite, limestone and other calcareous stone or cement, cement clinkers, and gypsum are subject to B7 product quality or performance requirement, A21 tolerance limits for residues of or contamination by certain (non-microbiological) substances, and B83 certification requirements.

Juice of fruit or vegetables, homogenous preparations, orange and apple juice, and citrus fruit juice are subject to A14 special authorization requirements for SPS reasons, A21 tolerance limits for residues of or contamination by certain (non-microbiological) substances, A22 restricted use of certain substances in foods and feeds and their contact materials, and A31 and B31 labeling requirements.

Table 7: Impediments while Exporting to Nepal

Products	Standards
Ferrosilicon and ferromanganese	Subject to NTMs such as B1 prohibitions or restrictions of imports, B7 product quality or performance requirement, and B83 certification requirement.
Portland cement, dolomite, limestone and other calcareous stone or cement, cement clinkers, and gypsum	Subject to B7 product quality or performance requirement, A21 tolerance limits for residues of or contamination by certain (non-microbiological) substances, and B83 certification requirements. B14 authorization requirement for TBT reasons is also required for these products.
Wire of refined copper	Subject to B7 product quality or performance requirement and B83 certification requirement.
Fruit juices	Subject to A14 special authorization requirements for SPS reasons, A21 tolerance limits for residues of or contamination by certain (non-microbiological) substances, A22 restricted use of certain substances in foods and feeds and their contact materials, and A31 and B31 labeling requirements.

NTM = nontariff measure, SPS = sanitary and phytosanitary, TBT = technical barrier to trade.
Source: Asian Development Bank consultant, based on interviews and desk research.

Procedural

As seen in Appendix 3, Table A3.3, no significant procedural obstacles have been observed in trade with Nepal. Bhutan exports gypsum anhydrite worth $871,157 per year to Nepal, accounting for close to 0.1% of Bhutan's total exports of the product. Bhutan also exports gypsum or calcined sulfate worth $9,302 per year and ferrosilicon worth $2,276 per year to Nepal.

Chapter 6
Prioritized Recommendations for Action

Based on the analysis and field work carried out for the Bhutan national diagnostic study, the recommendations presented in sections 6.1, 6.2, and 6.3 are grouped under three areas: legislation and regulatory frameworks, institutional frameworks, and infrastructure development.

Legislation and Regulatory Frameworks

Review and update legislation and regulatory frameworks. Bhutan should undertake a review process to ensure validity and consistency across frameworks. In particular, the review should seek to develop consistency between the Food Act and the Standards Act to prevent conflicting provisions.

Secure accreditation of domestic analytic laboratories. Bhutan should seek international accreditation for its laboratory facilities and test protocols—accreditation for BAFRA labs can address SPS barriers while accreditation for BSB labs can reduce TBTs. International accreditation would bring significant benefits by (i) enabling SPS and TBT certification issued in Bhutan to meet the import requirements of countries such as India, Bangladesh, and others; and (ii) ensuring the provision of competent analytical services, establishment of quality management and up-to-date standard operating procedures, and provision and use of adequate equipment.

Mutual recognition of certification. Bhutanese stakeholders should engage the relevant agencies involved in SPS and TBT certification in Bangladesh and India to develop mutual recognition agreements and equivalent inspection and certification systems.

Strengthen and expedite South Asian Regional Standards Organization operations and implementation. There is a pressing need to harmonize nontariff measures among trading partners in the subregion, which falls under the mandate of SARSO. Bhutan should also engage with regional counterparts to explore harmonization of conformity assessment.

Improve banking procedures and arrangements. Banking transactions between Bhutanese exporters and Bangladeshi importers should be improved to avoid long payment delays. Mutual understanding between banks and traders could help make terms and conditions of letters of credit more user-friendly and beneficial to both parties.

Regular review of transit agreements. Existing trade and transit agreements with India under the Agreement on Trade, Commerce and Transit (footnote 11) should be reviewed at regular intervals to address issues arising from issues encountered during everyday transit, including, including inadequate customs infrastructure, the limited number of entry and exit points, documentation requirements, and procedures and formalities.

Enhance sanitary and phytosanitary and technical barrier to trade dialogue and diplomacy with other SASEC countries. The 18-product sensitive list of Bangladesh should be discussed, negotiated, and expanded. For example, Bhutan exports juices to Bangladesh under the 18-product sensitive list under duty-free conditions, but only for canned and bottled products. Meanwhile, products in aseptic sterile packaging bear heavy customs duties of 25%, which renders trade uncompetitive.

Institutional Frameworks

Designate clear institutional mandates. Domestic authorities should review legislation to ensure it stipulates clear roles and responsibilities for institutions in standard setting, certification, laboratory testing, enforcement, and compliance. In particular, BAFRA should focus its operations on being a regulatory body rather than on setting standards. It should consider relinquishing certification mandates to prevent potential conflicts of interest inherent in having both standard setting and laboratory and certification responsibilities under a single management body. There is need for a clear policy to define distinct mandates between institutions, and BAFRA and the BSB should explore practical measures to help them effectively fulfill their respective mandates.

Strengthen sanitary and phytosanitary and technical barrier to trade agency coordination. Bhutan's National Transport and Trade Facilitation Committee (NTTFC), in particular, can enhance interagency cooperation. The NTTFC should encourage deeper collaboration between government agencies, as well as between public and private sector representatives, to support better understanding of the challenges of trade and business affected by SPS and TBT procedures and processes.

Build institutional skills and technical capacity. Develop laboratory, institutional, and technical capacity to meet international standards. Some suggested actions include the following:

(i) Conduct a comprehensive, coordinated, and in-depth review of human resources and technical skills across SPS and TBT agencies; establish a register that matches skills against strategic priorities and requirements; and develop targeted time-bound skills development programs in line with strategic priorities and agenda of the SPS and TBT agencies.
(ii) Conduct in-depth assessment of laboratory facilities and standard operating procedures, identify gaps, and develop action plans to address the shortfalls.
(iii) Seek sufficient annual budgetary allocations for capacity-building initiatives and required additional staff for BAFRA and the BSB at the senior technical and policy levels, as well as in the field offices.
(iv) Explore opportunities for trained technical staff (especially in highly specialized areas such as standard setting, metrology, testing, and certification) to remain in situ beyond standard rotations required by Bhutan's Royal Civil Service Commission.

Strengthen access to sanitary and phytosanitary and technical barriers to trade information and disseminate it better to the public and private sectors. Develop a centralized portal or database to improve dissemination of information on SPS and TBT notifications to all affected bodies in trade and business. Coordinate with Bhutan's NTTFC, chambers of commerce, and industry associations to identify practical solutions to the SPS- and TBT-related information gap.

Activate sanitary and phytosanitary and technical barriers to trade enquiry points. These enquiry points should be activated in relevant government agencies to assist in public–private sector relations, and the entire enquiry point system should be operationalized by reviewing and updating terms of reference and seeking the necessary resources.

Infrastructure Development

Physical infrastructure development. This is required for the following:

(i) **A new and separate Bhutan Standards Bureau metrology laboratory.** In its current location, vibration disturbances do not allow precise equipment calibration and testing at the lab. Establishing an independent laboratory will be necessary to address this issue.

(ii) **Plant quarantine facilities.** Adequate and efficient plant quarantine management and facilities are needed at the entry points of quarantine stations in Gelephu, Nganglam, Paro, Phuentsholing, and Samtse. Physical infrastructure upgrades should be complemented by capacity building for plant inspectors on technical knowledge such as detection techniques and identification of pests and diseases.

(iii) **Border-crossing facilities.** Upgrades are required, particularly to support more efficient and effective customs formalities and transport. Bhutan's industrial activities are concentrated in the south, where the major industrial estates and cross-border facilities are located. Existing border infrastructure will struggle to accommodate growing traffic flow and should be upgraded to support larger volumes.

Develop private sector engagement and explore investment partnership in sanitary and phytosanitary- and technical barrier to trade-related infrastructure. Explore the potential to engage the private sector investment to develop SPS- and TBT-related infrastructure at and behind the border. Utilize the public–private platform provided by Bhutan's NTTFC to initiate discussion and collaboration between the government and relevant chambers of commerce and industry associations.

Initiate regional discussions on developing regional infrastructure and facilities networks. These discussions should include sharing laboratory facilities between SASEC trading partners rather than duplicating laboratory and other facilities in each country. Establishing networks of regional laboratories without each country having to set up separate laboratories would be a resource-effective approach for all SASEC countries: for example, Bhutan could specialize in testing for organic agriculture and products.

Conduct a comprehensive inventory of sanitary and phytosanitary and technical barriers to trade infrastructure. This should include testing and analytical facilities in Bhutan and neighboring SASEC countries to prioritize domestic needs as well as regional opportunities for shared facility development.

Collaborate to upgrade infrastructure. Strengthen high-level bilateral and regional dialogue to upgrade infrastructure facilities, equipment, and procedures in other SASEC countries that negatively affect cross-border trade for Bhutan. The same collaborative approach should be applied on the domestic front for customs clearance infrastructure and services in terms of equipment (automation and information and communication technology); documentation procedures; vehicle traffic; loading and unloading areas; and vehicle bays.

Leverage government collaboration. Engage joint government commission structures and processes to address issues such as road strikes, customs infrastructure, increased entry and exit points for SPS and TBT cargoes, documentation, procedures, and formalities.

Develop human capacity in technical areas of sanitary and phytosanitary measures and technical barriers to trade. Strengthen technical capabilities to optimize the efficient use of SPS and TBT facilities and certification bodies. Technical expertise is currently inadequate in the areas of certification, calibration, metrology, and accreditation. Building capacity in these areas will require close collaboration with the human resource planning departments of the Royal Civil Service Commission. The first steps should focus on developing a comprehensive technical capacity register of existing skills, comparing it with the projected increase of infrastructure and facilities, and conducting a gap analysis. Human resource planning should be closely linked to facilities upgrading in SPS and TBT infrastructure.

Chapter 7
Conclusion

This study provides an overview of Bhutan's trade patterns with other SASEC countries, focusing on how SPS and TBT dynamics affect trade with Bangladesh, India, and, to a lesser extent, Nepal.

The study finds that Bhutan is similar to many developing economies in that it faces significant challenges in the areas of SPS and TBT. Core issues include inadequate infrastructure, old equipment, and young institutions that face skills shortages and limited human resources. These barriers challenge the implementation of SPS and TBT solutions to promote efficient trade.

More diverse and efficient trade is hindered by SPS and TBT measures, institutional practices, and legal frameworks. This study presents potential Bhutanese export products to India, Bangladesh, and Nepal—53 products for Bangladesh, 13 for India, and 101 for Nepal—that could be traded in greater volumes if SASEC countries address SBS and TBT bottlenecks.

Geographical proximity is a key factor for establishing and sustaining efficient trade. With India as Bhutan's immediate neighbor, 90% of Bhutan's trade (both imports and exports) is with India, and trade dominance with India is likely to persist. Another key determinant factor is preferential treatments through trade agreements. Bhutan enjoys free trade with India, with low tariffs that no other country can offer. Trade with Bangladesh is only competitive within the list of specific duty-free products—there are ongoing negotiations to replace products on the duty-free list with others that Bhutan is better equipped to export, or to increase the number from 18 to 100 products.

The study presents findings on trade partners and regimes, as well as options to diversify trade through SPS and TBT measures. It also discusses factors that facilitate trade and how to expand on trade facilitation dynamics, such as trade agreements, and more efficient certification and accreditation entities. The study recognizes the importance of SPS and trade regulations as safeguards to protect health and safety, but highlights ways in which they can be made more efficient to reduce barriers to more diverse and robust trade across the SASEC subregion.

Appendix 1
Top 10 Export and Import Products between Bhutan and Other SASEC Countries

Table A1.1: Top 10 Export Products to Bangladesh in 2015

Series No.	Harmonized System Code (6 Digits)	Description	Export Value ($ million)
1	090831	Cardamom (neither crushed nor ground)	8.567
2	080510	Oranges	6.766
3	252100	Limestone and other calcareous stone	4.727
4	251710	Pebbles, gravel, and boulders	1.306
5	080810	Apples	0.931
6	720712	Semifinished products of iron	0.713
7	251810	Dolomite, not calcified or sintered, lumps or slabs	0.601
8	252010	Gypsum	0.474
9	720221	Ferroalloys containing weight more than 55% silicon	0.298
10	283650	Calcium carbonate	0.298
	Total of top 10		24.681
	Share of top 10 in total export to Bangladesh		89.63%

Source: Government of Bhutan, Ministry of Finance, Department of Revenue and Customs. 2016. *Bhutan Trade Statistics 2015*. Thimphu.

Table A1.2: Top 10 Import Products from Bangladesh to Bhutan in 2015

Series No.	Harmonized System Code (6 Digits)	Description	Import Value ($ million)
1	732620	Articles of steel wire	0.39
2	200989	Mango juice	0.34
3	200989	Litchi juice	0.33
4	761010	Aluminum doors and windows	0.23
5	340111	Soap (toilet use)	0.09
6	300320	Antibiotics (medicine)	0.02
7	732010	Leaf springs of iron and steel	0.02
8	620332	Boy's cotton ware	0.02
9	870850	Drive's axles with differentials	0.02
10	841320	Hand pumps for liquids	0.17
	Total of top 10		1.63

Source: Government of Bhutan, Ministry of Finance, Department of Revenue and Customs. 2016. *Bhutan Trade Statistics 2015*. Thimphu.

Table A1.3: Top 10 Export Products to India in 2015 (Excluding Electricity)

Series No.	Harmonized System Code (6 Digits)	Description	Export Value ($ million)
1	720221	Ferroalloys	95.567
2	252329	Cement	38.840
3	720712	Semifinished products of iron	27.332
4	284920	Calcium carbide	24.479
5	251810	Dolomite	20.606
6	392020	Plastics (propylene, polymers, scrap plastics)	9.138
7	252010	Gypsum	8.383
8	070190	Edible vegetables	5.620
9	441011	Particle board	3.825
10	220710	Undenatured ethyl alcohol more than 80% strength	3.589
	Total of top 10		9
	Share of top 10 in total export to India		79.62%

Note: Numbers may not sum precisely because of rounding.
Source: Government of Bhutan, Ministry of Finance, Department of Revenue and Customs. 2016. *Bhutan Trade Statistics 2015*. Thimphu.

Table A1.4: Top 10 Import Products from India to Bhutan in 2015

Series No.	Harmonized System Code (6 Digits)	Description	Import Value ($ million)
1	271019	Other light oils (HSD)	80.95
2	841090	Hydraulic turbines, parts including regulators	50.69
3	271012	Motor spirit	26.03
4	730820	Towers and lattice masts (prefabricated building materials)	22.80
5	100630	Semi-milled rice	17.32
6	270410	Coke and semicoke	16.13
7	721410	Bars of iron rods	10.67
8	040210	Mill cream in powder, granules	8.18
9	020110	Carcasses of bovine	8.01
10	250610	Quartz	7.24
	Total of top 10		248.02

HSD = high-speed diesel.
Source: Government of Bhutan, Ministry of Finance, Department of Revenue and Customs. 2016. *Bhutan Trade Statistics 2015*. Thimphu.

Table A1.5: Top 10 Export Products to Nepal in 2015

Series No.	Harmonized System Code (6 Digits)	Description	Export Value ($ million)
1	252010	Gypsum anhydrite	0.942
2	270112	Coal	0.119
3	270400	Coke and semicoke	0.013
	Total of top 10		4
	Share of top 10 in total export to Nepal		87.92%

Note: Numbers may not sum precisely because of rounding.
Source: Government of Bhutan, Ministry of Finance, Department of Revenue and Customs. 2016. *Bhutan Trade Statistics 2015*. Thimphu.

Table A1.6: Top 10 Import Products from Nepal to Bhutan in 2015

Series No.	Harmonized System Code (6 Digits)	Description	Import Value ($ million)
1	830629	Plated with precious metal (others)	0.08
2	830621	Plated with precious metal	0.06
3	340130	Soap (toilet use)	0.05
4	190410	Prepared food stuffs	0.03
5	610130	Men/boys textile fiber	0.01
6	500790	Woven fabric tego	0.01
7	500790	Woven fabric wangju	0.01
8	500790	Woven fabric other	0.01
9	090110	Coffee non-decaffeinated	0.01
10	020443	Boneless meat of goat/sheep	0.01
	Total of top 10		0.28

Source: Government of Bhutan, Ministry of Finance, Department of Revenue and Customs. 2016. *Bhutan Trade Statistics 2015*. Thimphu.

Appendix 2
Potential Export Items from Bhutan to Other SASEC Countries

Table A2.1: Potential and Existing Export Products from Bhutan to Bangladesh
($)

Series No.	HS Code	Product Label	Average Annual Export of Bhutan	Average Unit Value of Export of Bhutan	Average Export of Bhutan to Bangladesh	Average Imports of Bangladesh from World	Average Unit Cost of Import of Bangladesh	Average Share of Import of Bangladesh from Bhutan	Average Share of Export to Bangladesh to Total Export of Bhutan
1	252329	Portland cement NES	24,668,656	0.042	2,173.11	2,626,958	0.112	0.00	0.00
2	721430	Bars and rods, including non-alloy steel, hot-rolled, drawn, or extruded	14,799,189	0.341	13,410.88	531,260	1.871	0.03	0.00
3	284910	Calcium carbide	14,347,663	0.405	0.00	1,434,866	0.650	0.00	0.00
4	740819	Wire of refined copper, maximum cross-sectional dimension less than or equal to 6 millimeters	11,919,995	2.540	0.00	872,438	7.059	0.00	0.00
5	252010	Gypsum; anhydrite	8,509,978	0.011	433,677.31	9,963,268	0.019	0.04	0.05
6	392099	Film and sheet, noncellular, of plastics NES	5,531,079	1.231	0.00	5,986,892	7.163	0.00	0.00
7	280469	Silicon NES	4,058,067	0.977	0.00	246,914	2.359	0.00	0.00
8	252310	Cement clinkers	2,952,224	0.032	0.00	354,287,648	0.048	0.00	0.00
9	720610	Ingots, iron, or non-alloy steel, of a purity of less than 99.94% iron	2,728,297	0.267	0.00	49,857	5.359	0.00	0.00
10	220710	Undenatured ethyl alcohol of strength by volume of 80% volume or higher	2,211,037	0.479	0.00	394,855	1.247	0.00	0.00
11	220210	Waters, including mineral and aerated	2,192,922	0.149	0.00	1,331,754	1.909	0.00	0.00
12	720299	Ferroalloys NES	2,117,862	1.599	0.00	102,271	3.452	0.00	0.00

continued on next page

Table A2.1 continued

Series No.	HS Code	Product Label	Average Annual Export of Bhutan	Average Unit Value of Export of Bhutan	Average Export of Bhutan to Bangladesh	Average Imports of Bangladesh from World	Average Unit Cost of Import of Bangladesh	Average Share of Import of Bangladesh from Bhutan	Average Share of Export to Bangladesh to Total Export of Bhutan
13	110100	Wheat or meslin flour	1,565,425	0.169	7,225.51	1,125,774	0.549	0.05	0.00
14	200989	Juice of fruit or vegetables, unfermented	1,039,487	0.250	1,521.64	141,120	1.472	0.02	0.01
15	252020	Plasters (consisting of calcined gypsum or calcium sulfate)	929,437	0.035	7,401.23	3,415,012	0.133	0.00	0.01
16	281122	Silicon dioxide	910,422	0.082	0.00	1,935,846	0.989	0.00	0.00
17	440290	Wood charcoal, including shell or nut charcoal	894,983	0.033	6,464.53	82,270	1.933	0.12	0.01
18	720410	Waste and scrap, cast iron	860,574	0.183	0.00	4,770,124	0.376	0.00	0.00
19	210610	Protein concentrates and textured protein substances	858,218	4.008	0.00	106,517	5.350	0.00	0.00
20	080290	Nuts edible, fresh or dried, whether or not shelled or peeled	704,914	0.294	2,826.15	31,023,320	1.005	0.00	0.00
21	091011	Ginger: Neither crushed nor ground	668,217	0.402	24327.36	36,390,040	0.661	0.00	0.03
22	720719	Semi-finished products, iron or non-alloy steel, counting by weight less than 0.25% carbon	667,959	0.264	0.00	171,647,264	0.642	0.00	0.00
23	220300	Beer made from malt	602,237	0.264	0.00	3,049,070	0.987	0.00	0.00
24	270119	Coal NES, whether or not pulverized, but not agglomerated	591,334	0.052	3,325.84	66,498,708	0.065	0.00	0.01
25	391740	Fittings, plastic	580,116	0.430	0.00	3,994,577	4.888	0.00	0.00
26	720229	Ferrosilicon NES	546,134	0.096	0.00	16,189	1.508	0.00	0.00
27	270600	Tar distilled from coal, lignite, or peat and other mineral tars	472,499	0.287	0.00	3,219,418	0.602	0.00	0.00
28	392321	Sacks and bags (including cones) of polymers of ethylene	409,029	0.732	0.00	14,318,083	6.786	0.00	0.00

continued on next page

Table A2.1 continued

Series No.	HS Code	Product Label	Average Annual Export of Bhutan	Average Unit Value of Export of Bhutan	Average Export of Bhutan to Bangladesh	Average Imports of Bangladesh from World	Average Unit Cost of Import of Bangladesh	Average Share of Import of Bangladesh from Bhutan	Average Share of Export to Bangladesh to Total Export of Bhutan
29	252210	Quicklime	337,438	0.024	0.00	1,779,235	0.174	0.00	0.00
30	261900	Slag, dross (excluding granulated slag), scaling and other waste	323,786	0.026	0.00	43,502	1.668	0.00	0.00
31	200911	Orange juice, unfermented and not spirited	292,469	0.336	2,092.70	189,554	1.863	0.01	0.01
32	441231	Plywood consisting solely of sheets of wood less than or equal to 6 millimeters thick	266,570	0.104	0.00	79,857	286.836	0.00	0.00
33	720430	Waste and scrap, of tinned iron or steel	259,113	0.120	0.00	11,308,374	0.293	0.00	0.00
34	701090	Carboys, bottles, flasks, jars, pots, phials, and other containers	229,632	0.025	0.00	13,401,035	1.280	0.00	0.00
35	391590	Plastics waste and scrap NES	223,399	0.081	0.00	1,343,484	0.738	0.00	0.00
36	210320	Tomato ketchup and other tomato sauces	208,625	0.376	34,977.42	263,362	0.807	0.14	0.17
37	220840	Rum and tafia	194,527	0.558	0.00	61,535	7.228	0.00	0.00
38	722100	Bars and rods, stainless steel, hot-rolled, in irregularly wound coils	185,317	0.144	0.00	34,270	2.717	0.00	0.00
39	200990	Mixtures of juices, unfermented and not spirited	181,740	0.276	5,647.15	178,473	0.895	0.03	0.01
40	470790	Waste and scrap of paper or paperboard	179,753	0.038	0.00	12,271,029	0.273	0.00	0.00
41	721320	Bars and rods, including non-alloy steel, hot-rolled, in irregular wound coils	168,541	0.305	0.00	1,435,959	0.688	0.00	0.00
42	800200	Tin waste and scrap	165,416	0.087	0.00	586,312	0.369	0.00	0.00
43	940360	Furniture, wooden, NES	164,952	23.751	0.00	5,918,556	102.698	0.00	0.00

continued on next page

Table A2.1 continued

Series No.	HS Code	Product Label	Average Annual Export of Bhutan	Average Unit Value of Export of Bhutan	Average Export of Bhutan to Bangladesh	Average Imports of Bangladesh from World	Average Unit Cost of Import of Bangladesh	Average Share of Import of Bangladesh from Bhutan	Average Share of Export to Bangladesh to Total Export of Bhutan
44	150790	Soybean oil and its fractions, refined	162,335	0.369	0.00	3,006,825	1.446	0.00	0.00
45	550912	Yarn containing greater than or equal to 85% nylon or other polyamide staple fibers	158,893	0.638	0.00	7,796,527	5.434	0.00	0.00
46	540234	Textured synthetic filament yarn of polypropylene	154,192	1.312	0.00	216,703	2.341	0.00	0.00
47	220830	Whiskies	151,854	0.706	0.00	4,945,171	8.236	0.00	0.00
48	271320	Petroleum bitumen	145,863	0.329	0.00	11,467,306	0.570	0.00	0.00
49	070610	Carrots and turnips, fresh or chilled	142,059	0.287	0.00	478,095	0.508	0.00	0.00
50	392329	Sacks and bags (including cones) of plastics NES	134,731	0.578	0.00	10,388,163	5.667	0.00	0.00
51	392350	Stoppers, lids, caps, and other closures of plastics	126,602	0.871	0.00	4,715,240	6.190	0.00	0.00
52	200919	Orange juice and NES, unfermented not spirited	124,155	0.308	0.00	94,305	0.649	0.00	0.00
53	540233	Textured yarn NES, of polyester filaments	109,878	0.448	0.00	106,608,744	2.077	0.00	0.00

HS = Harmonized System, NES = not elsewhere specified.

Source: Government of Bhutan, Ministry of Finance, Department of Revenue and Customs. 2016. *Bhutan Trade Statistics 2015*. Thimphu.

Table A2.2: Potential and Existing Export Products from Bhutan to India ($)

Series No.	HS Code	Product Label	Average Annual Export of Bhutan	Average Unit Value of Export of Bhutan	Average Export of Bhutan to India	Average Import of India from World	Average Unit Cost of Import of India	Average Share of Import of India from Bhutan	Average Share of Export to India to Total Export of Bhutan
1	080510	Oranges, fresh or dried	5,953,103	0.194	381,178	22,903,164	0.617	0.02	0.24
2	090830	Cardamoms	5,710,014	0.384	1,985,870	23,309,950	8.837	0.09	0.35
3	270112	Bituminous coal, whether or not pulverized not agglomerated	1,777,351	0.054	1,278,235	570,335,744	0.118	0.07	0.65
4	080810	Apples, fresh	1,461,623	0.232	682,545	207,506,400	1.081	0.00	0.48
5	252620	Natural steatite, crushed or powdered	477,378	0.028	283,069	2,220,145	0.761	0.14	0.61
6	251710	Pebbles, gravel, broken or crushed stone used for aggregates	476,733	0.007	116,526	16,189,236	0.020	0.01	0.55
7	283650	Calcium carbonate	260,160	0.080	12,011	85,207,816	0.148	0.00	0.04
8	270400	Coke and semicoke of coal, lignite or peat, agglomerated	94,722	0.087	61,375	740,046,784	0.231	0.00	0.52
9	200980	Fruit and vegetable juice NES (excluding mix) unfermented and unspirited	79,521	0.028	12,230	9,082,044	1.495	0.00	0.15
10	252610	Natural steatite, not crushed or powdered	54,953	0.020	26,326	194,510	0.375	0.13	0.57
11	100630	Rice, semi-milled or wholly milled	35,460	0.844		1,181,219	1.081	0.00	0.00
12	253090	Mineral substances, NES	27,912	0.113	3,548	14,487,011	0.125	0.00	0.33
13	200599	Vegetables and mixtures of vegetables, prepared	24,418	0.071	2,452	564,324	2.274	0.00	0.10

HS = Harmonized System, NES = not elsewhere specified.

Source: Government of Bhutan, Ministry of Finance, Department of Revenue and Customs. 2016. *Bhutan Trade Statistics 2015*. Thimphu.

Table A2.3: Potential and Existing Export Products from Bhutan to Nepal
($)

Series No.	HS Code	Product Label	Average Annual Export of Bhutan	Average Unit Value of Export of Bhutan	Average Export of Bhutan to Nepal	Average Import of Nepal from World	Average Unit Cost of Import of Nepal	Average Share of Nepal from World	Average Share of Export to Nepal to Total Export of Bhutan
1	720221	Ferrosilicon, containing by weight more than 55% of silicon	106,885,560	0.642	2,276	29,200	1.42	0.07	0
2	720712	Semifinished product, iron or non-alloy steel, (other than square cross section)	29,696,594	0.467		776,969	0.83	0.00	0
3	252329	Portland cement NES	24,668,656	0.042	-	34,939,652	0.08	0.00	0
4	251810	Dolomite not calcined or sintered	16,640,244	0.004	3,536	525,424	0.08	0.00	0
5	284910	Calcium carbide	14,347,663	0.405	-	363,285	0.70	0.00	0
6	721430	Bars and rods, iron or non-alloy steel, hot-rolled, drawn, or extruded of free-cutting steel	13,116,862	0.424	-	10,629	1.14	0.00	0
7	740819	Wire of refined copper, maximum cross-sectional dimension of less than or equal to 6 millimeters	11,919,995	2.540	-	4,802,999	6.12	0.00	0
8	252010	Gypsum; anhydrite	8,509,978	0.011	871,157	7,906,548	0.06	0.11	0.09
9	080510	Oranges, fresh or dried	5,953,103	0.194	-	2,467,246	0.25	0.00	0
10	070190	Potatoes, fresh or chilled NES	5,881,857	0.133	2,407	30,872,684	0.19	0.00	0
11	392099	Film and sheet, noncellular, of plastics NES	5,531,079	1.231	-	3,494,339	1.66	0.00	0
12	252100	Limestone flux; limestone and other calcareous stone, for lime or cement	4,932,807	0.030	859	32,728	0.10	0.02	0
13	280469	Silicon NES	4,058,067	0.977	-	101,129	1.58	0.00	0
14	252310	Cement clinkers	2,952,224	0.032	-	80,238,648	0.07	0.00	0

continued on next page

Table A2.3 continued

Series No.	HS Code	Product Label	Average Annual Export of Bhutan	Average Unit Value of Export of Bhutan	Average Export of Bhutan to Nepal	Average Import of Nepal from World	Average Unit Cost of Import of Nepal	Average Share of Nepal from World	Average Share of Export to Nepal to Total Export of Bhutan
15	220710	Undenatured ethyl alcohol of an alcohol strength by volume of 80% volume or higher	2,211,037	0.479	–	4,644,198	0.76	0.00	0
16	110100	Wheat or meslin flour	1,565,425	0.169	–	2,531,080	0.32	0.00	0
17	080810	Apples, fresh	1,461,623	0.232	–	15,998,079	0.34	0.00	0
18	200989	Juice of fruit or vegetables, unfermented	1,322,439	0.332	–	222,626	1.04	0.00	0
19	200710	Homogenized preparation (jams, fruit jellies)	1,284,782	0.307	–	77,319	1.27	0.00	0
20	252020	Plasters consisting of calcined gypsum or calcium sulfate	929,437	0.035	9,302	460,094	0.10	0.02	0.01
21	281122	Silicon dioxide	910,422	0.082	–	239,242	1.00	0.00	0
22	720410	Waste and scrap, cast iron	860,574	0.183	–	148,564	0.37	0.00	0
23	210610	Protein concentrates and textured protein substances	858,218	4.008	–	1,987,460	7.52	0.00	0
24	440290	Wood charcoal, including shell or nut charcoal, whether or not agglomerate	816,998	0.026	–	28,828	0.57	0.00	0
25	091011	Ginger: Neither crushed nor ground	794,168	0.535	–	835,259	3.05	0.00	0
26	080290	Nuts edible, fresh or dried, whether or not shelled or peeled, NES	704,914	0.294	–	33,748,200	0.86	0.00	0
27	720719	Semifinished product, iron or non-alloy steel, counting by weight less than 0.25% carbon, NES	667,959	0.264	–	253,139,648	0.57	0.00	0
28	220300	Beer made from malt	602,237	0.264	–	207,539	1.49	0.00	0
29	391740	Fittings, plastic	580,116	0.430	–	1,455,840	2.17	0.00	0
30	720229	Ferrosilicon, NES	564,117	0.077	–	23,168	1.30	0.00	0

continued on next page

Table A2.3 continued

Series No.	HS Code	Product Label	Average Annual Export of Bhutan	Average Unit Value of Export of Bhutan	Average Export of Bhutan to Nepal	Average Import of Nepal from World	Average Unit Cost of Import of Nepal	Average Share of Nepal from World	Average Share of Export to Nepal to Total Export of Bhutan
31	252620	Natural steatite, crushed or powdered	477,378	0.028	-	464,878	0.15	0.00	0
32	392321	Sacks and bags (including cones) of polymers of ethylene	409,029	0.732	-	232,804	3.83	0.00	0
33	252210	Quicklime	337,438	0.024	-	859,730	0.10	0.00	0
34	200911	Orange juice, unfermented and not spirited, whether or not sugared, sweet, or frozen	292,469	0.336	-	12,189	1.24	0.00	0
35	261900	Slag, dross (excluding granulated slag), scaling and other waste	289,168	0.041	-	1,112,250	0.08	0.00	0
36	441231	Plywood consisting solely of sheets of wood less than or equal to 6 millimeters thick	266,570	0.104	-	358,939	698.56	0.00	0
37	283650	Calcium carbonate	260,160	0.080	626	2,520,738	0.20	0.00	0
38	701090	Carboys, bottles, flasks, jars, pots, phials, and other containers	229,632	0.025	-	16,605,766	0.32	0.00	0
39	210320	Tomato ketchup and other tomato sauces	208,625	0.376	-	636,787	1.69	0.00	0
40	220840	Rum and tafia	194,527	0.558	-	68,499	8.54	0.00	0
41	470790	Waste and scrap of paper or paperboard, NES (including unsorted waste and scrap)	179,753	0.038	-	415,175	0.39	0.00	0
42	800200	Tin waste and scrap	165,416	0.087	-	10,046	4.35	0.00	0
43	940360	Furniture, wooden, NES	164,952	23.751	743	2,567,678	39.98	0.00	0.01
44	150790	Soybean oil and its fractions, refined but not chemically modified	162,335	0.369	-	1,504,669	1.31	0.00	0

continued on next page

Table A2.3 continued

Series No.	HS Code	Product Label	Average Annual Export of Bhutan	Average Unit Value of Export of Bhutan	Average Export of Bhutan to Nepal	Average Import of Nepal from World	Average Unit Cost of Import of Nepal	Average Share of Nepal from World	Average Share of Export to Nepal to Total Export of Bhutan
45	540234	Textured synthetic filament yarn of polypropylene (excluding sewing thread)	154,192	1.312	-	10,099	2.53	0.00	0
46	220830	Whiskies	151,854	0.706	-	6,465,525	11.61	0.00	0
47	271320	Petroleum bitumen	145,863	0.329	-	14,679,897	0.66	0.00	0
48	392329	Sacks and bags (including cones) of plastics NES	134,731	0.578	-	695,828	0.90	0.00	0
49	250620	Quartzite, merely cut, by sawing or otherwise, in blocks or slabs of a rectangular (including square) shape	129,106	0.003	-	29,830	0.12	0.00	0
50	200919	Orange juice and NES, unfermented not spirited, whether or not sugared or sweet	124,155	0.308	-	39,941	0.95	0.00	0
51	540233	Textured yarn NES, of polyester filaments, not put up for retail sale	109,878	0.448	-	967,450	2.09	0.00	0
52	071340	Lentils dried, shelled, whether or not skinned or split	93,382	0.574	-	13,453,211	0.66	0.00	0
53	391729	Tubes, pipes and hoses, rigid; of plastics NES	90,627	0.089	-	788,975	1.69	0.00	0
54	441294	Veneered panels and similar laminated wood with blockboard, laminboard	85,806	0.635	-	65,851	1.30	0.00	0
55	071010	Potatoes, frozen	82,232	0.125	-	499,653	0.17	0.00	0
56	220720	Ethyl alcohol and other spirits, denatured, of any strength	79,369	0.539	-	28,651	29.03	0.00	0
57	760200	Waste and scrap, aluminum	77,795	0.448	-	6,289,786	1.67	0.00	0
58	284990	Carbides NES	76,671	0.031	-	36,348	3.68	0.00	0
59	091099	Spices NES	75,911	0.267	-	1,888,026	0.93	0.00	0

continued on next page

Table A2.3 continued

Series No.	HS Code	Product Label	Average Annual Export of Bhutan	Average Unit Value of Export of Bhutan	Average Export of Bhutan to Nepal	Average Import of Nepal from World	Average Unit Cost of Import of Nepal	Average Share of Nepal from World	Average Share of Export to Nepal to Total Export of Bhutan
60	261800	Granulated slag (slag sand) from the manufacture of iron or steel	72,241	0.025	-	11,242,229	0.03	0.00	0
61	220110	Mineral and aerated waters not counting sugar or sweetening matter nor flavored	68,719	0.253	-	54,533	0.31	0.00	0
62	441232	Plywood of sheets of wood less than or equal to 6 millimeters thick	65,981	1.924	-	220,764	689.36	0.00	0
63	220890	Undenatured ethyl alcohol less than 80% alcohol content by volume and spirit, liqueur and spirit beverage NES	59,918	0.649	-	353,224	7.96	0.00	0
64	200971	Apple juice, unfermented, Brix value less than or equal to 20 at 20 degrees Celsius, whether or not concentrate	58,798	0.371	-	21,459	0.86	0.00	0
65	110311	Wheat groats and meal	57,369	0.161	-	656,742	0.32	0.00	0
66	220900	Vinegar and substitutes for vinegar obtained from acetic acid	55,918	0.207	-	22,936	1.10	0.00	0
67	252610	Natural steatite, not crushed or powdered	54,953	0.020	-	30,884	0.15	0.00	0
68	340119	Soap and organic surface-active products and preparations for use as soap, shaped, NES; papers and nonwovens impregnated with soap or preparation, NES	50,689	0.254	567	755,904	1.24	0.00	0.01

continued on next page

Table A2.3 continued

Series No.	HS Code	Product Label	Average Annual Export of Bhutan	Average Unit Value of Export of Bhutan	Average Export of Bhutan to Nepal	Average Import of Nepal from World	Average Unit Cost of Import of Nepal	Average Share of Nepal from World	Average Share of Export to Nepal to Total Export of Bhutan
69	200912	Orange juice, unfermented, Brix value of less than or equal to 20 at 20 degrees Celsius, whether or not concentrate	49,200	0.442	-	16,673	1.03	0.00	0
70	280440	Oxygen	47,533	0.090	-	150,433	0.24	0.00	0
71	940350	Bedroom furniture, wooden, NES	43,635	30.220	-	382,209	55.54	0.00	0
72	040120	Milk, not concentrated and unsweetened, exceeding 1% but not exceeding 6% fat	43,068	0.409	-	2,380,747	0.49	0.00	0
73	391731	Tubes, pipes and hoses, flexible, plastic, minimum burst pressure of 27.6 megapascals	41,115	0.501	-	135,735	2.48	0.00	0
74	740400	Waste and scrap, copper or copper alloy	39,224	1.889	-	11,691,905	6.02	0.00	0
75	732611	Balls, grinding, and similar articles for mills, forged or stamped but not further worked	38,005	0.785	-	376,491	1.03	0.00	0
76	481940	Sacks and bags, of paper, NES, including cones	37,940	0.287	-	238,261	1.24	0.00	0
77	401220	Pneumatic tires, used	37,208	0.756	-	22,543	17.42	0.00	0
78	740313	Billets, copper, unwrought	33,493	0.424	-	40,137	0.68	0.00	0
79	720230	Ferro-silico-manganese	33,327	0.382	-	1,925,591	1.05	0.00	0
80	230990	Animal feed preparations NES	32,162	0.104	-	20,280,844	0.94	0.00	0
81	441820	Doors and their frames and thresholds, of wood	31,843	0.346	-	1,260,418	0.73	0.00	0

continued on next page

Table A2.3 continued

Series No.	HS Code	Product Label	Average Annual Export of Bhutan	Average Unit Value of Export of Bhutan	Average Export of Bhutan to Nepal	Average Import of Nepal from World	Average Unit Cost of Import of Nepal	Average Share of Nepal from World	Average Share of Export to Nepal to Total Export of Bhutan
82	200791	Citrus fruit (marmalade, purée) obtained by cooking preparation whether or not sugared or sweetened	29,785	0.461	-	30,980	1.44	0.00	0
83	271099	Other waste oils	28,987	0.197	-	56,147	2.47	0.00	0
84	722860	Bars and rods of alloy steel (other than stainless), others, NES	28,433	0.173	-	70,192	1.07	0.00	0
85	130239	Mucilages and thickeners NES, modified or not, derived from vegetable products	28,391	1.064	-	25,233	3.38	0.00	0
86	270799	Oils and other products of the distillation of high-temperature coal tar. NES	24,163	0.360	-	175,160	0.68	0.00	0
87	401700	Hard rubber in all forms, including waste and scrap	23,489	0.108	-	92,161	11.64	0.00	0
88	200931	Single citrus fruit juice, unfermented, Brix value less than or equal to 20 at 20 degrees Celsius, whether or not containing added sugar or other sweetening matter	22,456	0.515	-	113,979	1.60	0.00	0
89	850710	Lead-acid electric accumulators of a kind used for starting piston engines	21,851	8.128	-	9,623,212	38.90	0.00	0
90	490199	Books, brochures, leaflets, and similar printed matter, NES	18,833	1.567	-	4,912,436	9.84	0.00	0
91	220850	Gin and geneva	17,985	1.051	-	1,391,192	11.90	0.00	0

continued on next page

Table A2.3 continued

Series No.	HS Code	Product Label	Average Annual Export of Bhutan	Average Unit Value of Export of Bhutan	Average Export of Bhutan to Nepal	Average Import of Nepal from World	Average Unit Cost of Import of Nepal	Average Share of Nepal from World	Average Share of Export to Nepal to Total Export of Bhutan
92	090411	Pepper of the genus *Piper*; dried or crushed or ground fruits of the genus *Capsicum* or of the genus *Pimenta*	17,066	0.330	–	8,230,873	6.18	0.00	0
93	392330	Carboys, bottles, flasks, and similar articles of plastics	17,021	0.265	–	4,101,329	1.14	0.00	0
94	732591	Balls, grinding, and similar articles of iron or steel, cast for mills	16,492	0.695	–	1,335,919	1.11	0.00	0
95	392390	Articles for the conveyance or packing of goods NES, of plastics	14,120	0.559	–	1,419,282	0.63	0.00	0
96	210310	Soy sauce	13,318	0.431	–	363,540	0.84	0.00	0
97	320300	Coloring matter of vegetable or animal origin and preparations based thereon	12,786	0.142	–	42,827	5.61	0.00	0
98	521214	Woven fabrics of cotton, less than or equal to 200 grams per square meter, of yarns of different colors, NES	11,483	2.088	–	1,803,643	39.11	0.00	0
99	830990	Stoppers, caps, lids, seals, and other packing accessories of base metal, NES	11,136	1.907	–	1,296,933	7.00	0.00	0
100	440349	Logs, tropical hardwoods NES	11,091	62.379	–	385,819	281.34	0.00	0
101	440799	Lumber, non-coniferous NES	10,530	1.892	–	1,347,848	73.16	0.00	0

HS = Harmonized System, NES = not elsewhere specified.

Sources: Government of Bhutan, Ministry of Finance, Department of Revenue and Customs. 2016. Bhutan Trade Statistics 2015. Thimphu; and United Nations. United Nations Comtrade Database (accessed August 2017).

Appendix 3
Existing Gaps in Standards and Regulations, Sanitary and Phytosanitary and Technical Barriers to Trade Measures, and Procedural Obstacles

Table A3.1: Existing Gaps in the Bangladesh Market

Series No. (1)	HS Code (2)	Description (3)	SPS and TBT Measures of Bhutan (4)	Details of SPS and TBT Agency of Bhutan (5)	SPS and TBT Measures of Bangladesh (6)	Details of SPS and TBT Agency of Bangladesh (7)	Details of Procedural Obstacles in Bhutan (8)	Details of Procedural Obstacles in Bangladesh (9)
1	252329	Portland cement NES	Product Brand Approval Scheme 2010 based on identical adoption of standards of the Bureau of Indian Standards; this involves mandatory health, safety, health, and environmental concerns. BTS IS 269: 1989 2004. OPC 33, 43, 53 grade	BSB Sales Tax, Customs and Excise Act, 2000	Import is subject to submission of a certificate from BSTI to the customs authority B83: Certification requirement	Import Policy Order, 2012–2015. VAT Act, 1991 and Customs Act, 1969 Ministry of Commerce National Board of Revenue Protection of domestic industries with no duty exemption	Lengthy documentation for exports (e.g., invoicing, trans-shipment) at border customs offices of India and Bangladesh	Banking transaction delays and inconveniences Longer distance to markets as compared to markets in border towns of India
2	721430	Bars and rods, or iron or non-alloy steel, hot-rolled, drawn or extruded of free-cutting steel, NES	Product Brand Approval Scheme 2010 based on identical adoption of standards of the Bureau of Indian Standards; this involves mandatory health, safety, health, and environmental concerns BTS IS 1786:2008, 2013	BSB Sales Tax, Customs and Excise Act, 2000.	Import is subject to submission of a certificate from BSTI to the customs authority Import Policy Order, 2012–2015	Import Policy Order, 2012–2015 Ministry of Commerce National Board of Revenue	Cross-border transshipment hassles	Banking transaction delays and inconveniences Longer distance to markets as compared to markets in border towns of India

continued on next page

Table A3.1 continued

Series No. (1)	HS Code (2)	Description (3)	SPS and TBT Measures of Bhutan (4)	Details of SPS and TBT Agency of Bhutan (5)	SPS and TBT Measures of Bangladesh (6)	Details of SPS and TBT Agency of Bangladesh (7)	Details of Procedural Obstacles in Bhutan (8)	Details of Procedural Obstacles in Bangladesh (9)
3	284910	Calcium carbide	No clear TBT measures identified	BSB Sales Tax, Customs and Excise Act, 2000	Import is subject to submission of a certificate from BSTI to the customs authority Import Policy Order, 2012–2015	Import Policy Order, 2012–2015 Ministry of Commerce National Board of Revenue	Border trans-shipment and payment delays	HS code discrepancies in the past Export not allowed except with the prior approval of the chief inspector of explosives of the Ministry of Power, Energy and Mineral Resources
4	740819	Wire of refined copper of which the maximum cross-sectional dimension is less than or equal to 6 millimeters	No clear TBT measures identified	BSB Sales Tax, Customs and Excise Act, 2000	TBT measures not known	Import Policy Order, 2012–2015 Ministry of Commerce National Board of Revenue	Cross-border transshipment hassles	Banking transaction delays and inconveniences Longer distance to markets as compared to markets in border towns of India
5	252010	Gypsum; anhydrite	No TBT measures identified	BSB	TBT measures not known	Import Policy Order, 2012–2015	Border trans-shipment delays Payment delays	Banking transaction delays and inconveniences Longer distance to markets as compared to markets in border towns of India
6	392099	Film and sheet., noncellular, of plastics NES	B14 authorization requirements for TBT reasons, E111 licensing procedure with no specific ex ante criteria	BSB Sales Tax, Customs and Excise Act, 2000	TBT measures not known	Ministry of Commerce National Board of Revenue	Border trans-shipment delays Payment delays	Polythene sheets with labels as per customer specifications sold to neighboring Indian companies only There are many industries in Bangladesh that do the same business supported by policies that protect the interests of domestic industries through tariff protection of 36%

continued on next page

Table A3.1 continued

Series No. (1)	HS Code (2)	Description (3)	SPS and TBT Measures of Bhutan (4)	Details of SPS and TBT Agency of Bhutan (5)	SPS and TBT Measures of Bangladesh (6)	Details of SPS and TBT Agency of Bangladesh (7)	Details of Procedural Obstacles in Bhutan (8)	Details of Procedural Obstacles in Bangladesh (9)
7	280469	Silicon NES	No TBT measures identified	BSB Sales Tax, Customs and Excise Act, 2000	TBT measures not identified	Ministry of Commerce National Board of Revenue	Border trans-shipment delays Payment delays	Banking transaction delays and inconveniences Longer distance to markets as compared to markets in border towns of India
8	252310	Cement clinkers	No clear TBT measures identified	BSB Sales Tax, Customs and Excise Act, 2000	Import subject to submission of a certificate from BSTI Import Policy Order, 2012–2015 VAT Act, 1991 and Customs Act, 1969	Import Policy Order, 2012–2015 Ministry of Commerce National Board of Revenue	Long distance to transport as compared to Indian markets	Border transfer hassles, payment delays
9	720610	Ingots, iron, or non-alloy steel, of a purity of less than 99.94% iron	No clear TBT measures identified	BSB Sales Tax, Customs and Excise Act, 2000	TBT measures not known	Only recognized bona fide user mills will import iron and steel Import Policy Order, 2012–2015	Cross-border transaction cost is high	Banking transaction delays and inconveniences Longer distance to markets as compared to markets in border towns of India
10	220710	Undenatured ethyl alcohol of an alcohol strength by volume of 80% volume or higher	A83 certification requirements A21 tolerance limits for residues of or contamination by certain non-microbiologic substances	BSB DOT, MOEA Sales Tax, Customs and Excise Act, 2000	E321: Prohibition for religious, moral or cultural reasons G332: Importers' own foreign exchange F69: Additional charges	Import Policy Order, 2012–2015 VAT Act, 1991 and Customs Act, 1969 Ministry of Commerce National Board of Revenue	High cross-border transaction costs for Indian roads and trucks	Cultural sensitivities and prohibitions

continued on next page

Table A3.1 continued

Series No. (1)	HS Code (2)	Description (3)	SPS and TBT Measures of Bhutan (4)	Details of SPS and TBT Agency of Bhutan (5)	SPS and TBT Measures of Bangladesh (6)	Details of SPS and TBT Agency of Bangladesh (7)	Details of Procedural Obstacles in Bhutan (8)	Details of Procedural Obstacles in Bangladesh (9)
11	220210	Waters, including mineral and aerated, containing sugar or sweetening matter or flavored	A83 and A84 certification and inspection requirements.	BAFRA BSB DOT, MOEA Sales Tax, Customs and Excise Act, 2000	B83 certification requirement Import is subject to submission of a certificate from BSTI to the customs authority	Import Policy Order, 2012–2015 Ministry of Commerce National Board of Revenue	Demands certification outside BSB and BAFRA, like ISI	Banking transaction delays based on current exports Longer distance to markets as compared to markets in border towns of India
12	720299	Ferroalloys, NES	No clear TBT measures identified	BSB DOT, MOEA Sales Tax, Customs and Excise Act, 2000	B7: Product quality or performance requirement C1: Pre-shipment inspection	Ministry of Commerce Import Policy Order, 2012–2015	Banking transactions inefficient and unreliable, and cause delays in fund transfer Border customs clearance delays, slow internet speed	Banking transactions delays based on current exports Longer distance to markets as compared to markets in border towns of India
13	110100	Wheat or meslin flour	A83 certification requirements	BAFRA BSB DOT, MOEA Sales Tax, Customs and Excise Act, 2000	A22: Restricted use of certain substances in foods and feeds and their contact materials A31: Labeling requirements A33: Packaging requirements A82: Testing requirement, including radioactivity levels test A83: Certification requirement (certification of radioactivity levels and certification that the food is fit for human consumption as well as certification from BSTI to the customs authority to the effect that the standard of the goods conforms to the Bangladeshi standard BDS-513:2002)	Import Policy Order, 2012–2015 Ministry of Commerce	Strong lobby to protect the domestic flour industry by Bangladesh Flour Mill Association	Banking transactions delays based on current exports Longer distance to markets as compared to markets in border towns of India

continued on next page

Table A3.1 continued

Series No. (1)	HS Code (2)	Description (3)	SPS and TBT Measures of Bhutan (4)	Details of SPS and TBT Agency of Bhutan (5)	SPS and TBT Measures of Bangladesh (6)	Details of SPS and TBT Agency of Bangladesh (7)	Details of Procedural Obstacles in Bhutan (8)	Details of Procedural Obstacles in Bangladesh (9)
14	200989	Juice of fruit or vegetables, unfermented, whether or not containing added sugar	B14: Authorization requirements for TBT A84: Inspection requirements Jam, jelly, and marmalade--drafting of national standards ongoing	BAFRA, Food Act, 2005 DOT, MOEA Sales Tax, Customs and Excise Act, 2000	A22: Restricted use of certain substances in foods and feeds and their contact materials A31: Labeling requirements A33: Packaging requirements) A82: Testing requirement, including radioactivity levels test A83: Certification requirement (certification of radioactivity levels and certification that the food is fit for human consumption as well as certification from BSTI to the customs authority to the effect that the standard of the goods conform to the Bangladeshi standard BDS-513:2002)	National Revenue Board Ministry of Commerce	Banking delays, border crossing complexities, requires third country certification BAFRA certificate not recognized	Banking transactions delays based on current exports Longer distance to markets as compared to markets in border towns of India Fit for human consumption certificate, which was not required in the past, causes delays
15	252020	Plasters (consisting of calcined gypsum or calcium sulfate)	No TBT measures identified	BSB DOT, MOEA Sales Tax, Customs and Excise Act, 2000		Import Policy Order, 2012–2015 Ministry of Commerce	Not known	Not known
16	281122	Silicon dioxide	No TBT measures identified	BSB DOT, MOEA Sales Tax, Customs and Excise Act, 2000	No known SPS and/or TBT measures	No known SPS and/or TBT measures	Not known	Banking transactions delays based on current exports Longer distance to markets as compared to markets in border towns of India

continued on next page

Appendix 3

Table A3.1 continued

Series No. (1)	HS Code (2)	Description (3)	SPS and TBT Measures of Bhutan (4)	Details of SPS and TBT Agency of Bhutan (5)	SPS and TBT Measures of Bangladesh (6)	Details of SPS and TBT Agency of Bangladesh (7)	Details of Procedural Obstacles in Bhutan (8)	Details of Procedural Obstacles in Bangladesh (9)
17	440290	Wood charcoal, including shell or nut charcoal	No TBT measures identified	BSB	No known SPS and/or TBT measures	No known SPS and/or TBT measures	Not known	Banking transactions delays based on current exports Longer distance to markets as compared to markets in border towns of India
18	720410	Waste and scrap, cast iron	No TBT measures identified	BSB	Prohibitions or restrictions of imports for objectives set out in the TBT agreement Only recognized bona fide user mills will import iron and steel Import Policy, 2012–2015	Import Policy Order 2012-2015 Ministry of Commerce	Not known	Banking transactions delays based on current exports. Longer distance to markets as compared to markets in border towns of India.
19	210610	Protein concentrates and textured protein substances	B14: Authorization requirement for TBT reasons, labeling requirements.	BAFRA	B83: Certification requirement (in case of import of protein concentrate prepared from bone meal, meat meal, and meat and bone meal from the United States, European and other countries)	Import Policy Order, 2012–2015 Ministry of Commerce	Not known	Banking transactions delays based on current exports Longer distance to markets as compared to markets in border towns of India
20	080290	Nuts edible, fresh or dried, whether or not shelled or peeled, NES	No SPS measures identified	BAFRA	No known SPS and/or TBT measures	No known SPS and/or TBT measures	Not known	Banking transactions delays based on current exports Longer distance to markets as compared to markets in border towns of India High tariff protection with customs duties 25%, supplementary tax 30%, value-added tax 15%, others 13%, and total 105.29%

continued on next page

Table A3.1 continued

Series No. (1)	HS Code (2)	Description (3)	SPS and TBT Measures of Bhutan (4)	Details of SPS and TBT Agency of Bhutan (5)	SPS and TBT Measures of Bangladesh (6)	Details of SPS and TBT Agency of Bangladesh (7)	Details of Procedural Obstacles in Bhutan (8)	Details of Procedural Obstacles in Bangladesh (9)
21	091011	Ginger: Neither crushed nor ground	BAFRA food safety standards	BAFRA	A22: Restricted use of certain substances in foods and feeds and their contact materials A82: Testing requirement A83: Certification requirement (radioactivity test reports and certification that food is fit for human consumption)	Import Policy Order, 2012–2015 Ministry of Commerce	Banking delays, border crossing complexities, requires third country certification	Fit for human consumption certificate, which was note required in the past, causes delays
22	720719	Semifinished product, iron or non-alloy steel, counting by weight less than 0.25% carbon, NES	No TBT measures identified	BSB DOT, MOEA Sales Tax, Customs and Excise Act, 2000	No TBT measures identified	Import Policy Order, 2012–2015 Ministry of Commerce VAT Act, 1991 and Customs Act, 1969	Banking delays, border crossing complexities, requires third country certification	Banking transactions delays based on current exports Longer distance to markets as compared to markets in border towns of India
23	220300	Beer made from malt	E121: Special authorization requirements for religious, cultural, or moral reasons A83, A84 for certification and inspection requirements.	BSB BAFRA DOT, MOEA Sales Tax, Customs and Excise Act, 2000	E321: Prohibition for religious, moral, or cultural reasons G332: Importers' own foreign exchange F69: Additional charges NES	Import Policy Order, 2012–2015 Ministry of Commerce VAT Act, 1991 and Customs Act, 1969	Banking delays, border crossing complexities, requires third country certification	Exports to neighboring Indian states, taking advantage of proximity and lower freight charges
24	270119	Coal NES, whether or not pulverized but not agglomerated	B14: Authorization requirements for TBT reasons E111: Licensing procedure with no specific ex ante criteria	BSB	No TBT measures identified	Import Policy Order, 2012–2015 Ministry of Commerce VAT Act, 1991 and Customs Act, 1969	Banking delay	Banking transactions delays based on current exports Longer distance to markets as compared to markets in border towns of India

continued on next page

Table A3.1 continued

Series No. (1)	HS Code (2)	Description (3)	SPS and TBT Measures of Bhutan (4)	Details of SPS and TBT Agency of Bhutan (5)	SPS and TBT Measures of Bangladesh (6)	Details of SPS and TBT Agency of Bangladesh (7)	Details of Procedural Obstacles in Bhutan (8)	Details of Procedural Obstacles in Bangladesh (9)
25	391740	Fittings, plastic	B14: Authorization requirements for TBT reasons E111: Licensing procedure with no specific ex ante criteria	BSB	No TBT measures identified			Banking transactions delays based on current exports Longer distance to markets as compared to markets in border towns of India
26	720229	Ferrosilicon, NES by weight less than or equal to 55% silicon	A83: Certification requirements.	DOT, MOEA		Import Policy Order, 2012–2015 Ministry of Commerce VAT Act, 1991 and Customs Act, 1969		Not exported to Bangladesh but sold entirely to Indian markets arising from proximity
27	270600	Tar distilled from coal, lignite, or peat and other mineral tars	B14: Authorization requirements for TBT reasons E111: Licensing procedure with no specific ex ante criteria	BSB		Import Policy Order, 2012–2015 Ministry of Commerce VAT Act, 1991 and Customs Act, 1969		Banking transactions delays based on current exports Longer distance to markets as compared to markets in border towns of India
28	392321	Sacks and bags (including cones) of polymers of ethylene	B14: Authorization requirements for TBT reasons E111: Licensing procedure with no specific ex ante criteria	BSB BAFRA DOT, MOEA	No SPS and TBT measures identified	Import Policy Order, 2012–2015 Ministry of Commerce National Board of Revenue		Banking transactions delays based on current exports Longer distance to markets as compared to markets in border towns of India

continued on next page

Table A3.1 continued

Series No. (1)	HS Code (2)	Description (3)	SPS and TBT Measures of Bhutan (4)	Details of SPS and TBT Agency of Bhutan (5)	SPS and TBT Measures of Bangladesh (6)	Details of SPS and TBT Agency of Bangladesh (7)	Details of Procedural Obstacles in Bhutan (8)	Details of Procedural Obstacles in Bangladesh (9)
29	252210	Quicklime		DOT, MOEA Sales Tax, Customs and Excise Act, 2000		Import Policy Order, 2012–2015 Ministry of Commerce National Board of Revenue		All exports to India, with exports in 2016 hitting Nu14.82 million Profitability and free trade; Bangladesh charges 30% duty Customs duties 5%, value-added tax 15%, others 9%, total 30%
30	261900	Slag, dross (excluding granulated slag), scaling and other waste	No TBT measures identified			Import Policy Order, 2012–2015 Ministry of Commerce National Board of Revenue		Only a minimal amount is available, as most is recycled as raw material for iron rods manufacturing
31	200911	Frozen orange juice, unfermented and not spirited, whether not sugared or sweet	B14: Authorization requirements for TBT reasons A83: Certification requirements BAFRA proposal to develop orange juice standards with Bhutan as the lead agency under SARSO	BAFRA DOT, MOEA Sales Tax, Customs and Excise Act, 2000	A22: Restricted use of certain substances in foods and feeds and their contact materials A31: Labeling requirements A33: Packaging requirements A82: Testing requirement including radioactivity levels test A83: Certification requirement (certification of radioactivity levels and that the food is fit for human consumption, as well as certification from BSTI to the customs authority to the effect that the standard of the goods conform to the Bangladeshi standard BDS- 513:2002)	Import Policy Order, 2012–2015 Ministry of Commerce		Fit for human consumption certificate causes huge delays prior to export

continued on next page

Appendix 3 69

Table A3.1 continued

Series No. (1)	HS Code (2)	Description (3)	SPS and TBT Measures of Bhutan (4)	Details of SPS and TBT Agency of Bhutan (5)	SPS and TBT Measures of Bangladesh (6)	Details of SPS and TBT Agency of Bangladesh (7)	Details of Procedural Obstacles in Bhutan (8)	Details of Procedural Obstacles in Bangladesh (9)
32	441231	Plywood consisting solely of sheets of wood less than or equal to 6 millimeters thick	BSB recognizes certified Indian Standards Institute 12823 BTS 13 3087, BTS IS 12823, BTS IS 2389, BTS IS 707, BTS IS 848, BTS IS 1374	BSB DOT, MOEA Sales Tax, Customs and Excise Act, 2000	TBT measures not identified	Import Policy Order, 2012–2015 Ministry of Commerce National Board of Revenue	Not known	Banking transactions delays based on current exports Longer distance to markets as compared to markets in border towns of India
33	720430	Waste and scrap, of tinned iron or steel	No TBT measures identified	BSB	B19: Prohibitions or restrictions of imports for objectives set out in the TBT agreement; only recognized bona fide user industrial unit shall be allowed to import iron and steel waste and scrap	Import Policy Order, 2012–2015 Ministry of Commerce	Not known	Not known
34	701090	Carboys, bottles, flasks, jars, pots, phials, and other containers	No SPS and TBT measures identified	BSB and BAFRA	B83: Certification requirement; a health certificate to the effect that the containers are fit for human use, issued by the appropriate authority of the exporting country, is required	Import Policy Order, 2012–2015 Ministry of Commerce	Not known	Not known
35	391590	Plastics waste and scrap NES	No SPS and TBT measures identified	BSB and BAFRA DOT, MOEA	SPS and TBT measures not identified	Import Policy Order, 2012–2015 Ministry of Commerce National Board of Revenue	Not known	Not known
36	210320	Tomato ketchup and other tomato sauces	B14: Authorization requirement for TBT reasons, labeling requirements	BAFRA Sales Tax, Customs and Excise Act, 2000	B83: Certification	Import Policy, 2012–2015 Ministry of Commerce		

continued on next page

Table A3.1 continued

Series No. (1)	HS Code (2)	Description (3)	SPS and TBT Measures of Bhutan (4)	Details of SPS and TBT Agency of Bhutan (5)	SPS and TBT Measures of Bangladesh (6)	Details of SPS and TBT Agency of Bangladesh (7)	Details of Procedural Obstacles in Bhutan (8)	Details of Procedural Obstacles in Bangladesh (9)
37	220840	Rum and tafia	B14: Authorization requirement for TBT reasons, labeling requirements	Sales Tax, Customs and Excise Act, 2000		Import Policy Order, 2012–2015; VAT Act, 1991; and Customs Act, 1969 No exports to Bangladesh because of religious, cultural, and moral reasons		
38	722100	Bars and rods, stainless steel, hot-rolled in irregularly wound coils	A83: Certification B14: Authorization requirement for TBT reasons, labeling requirements	BSB DOT, MOEA		No SPS and TBT standards identified	Not known	Not known
39	200990	Mixtures of juices, unfermented and not spirited, whether or not sugared or sweet	B14: Authorization requirement for TBT reasons, labeling requirements	BSB DOT, MOEA Sales Tax, Customs and Excise Act, 2000	A22: Restricted use of certain substances in foods and feeds and their contact materials A31: Labeling requirements A33: Packaging requirements A82: Testing requirement, including radioactivity levels test A83: Certification requirement (certification of radioactivity levels and certification that the food is fit for human consumption as well as certification from BSTI to the customs authority to the effect that the standard of the goods conform to the Bangladesh standard BDS-513:2002)	Import Policy Order, 2012–2015; VAT Act, 1991; and Customs Act, 1969 Ministry of Commerce		Banking transactions delays based on current exports Longer distance to markets as compared to markets in border towns of India

continued on next page

Appendix 3

Table A3.1 continued

Series No. (1)	HS Code (2)	Description (3)	SPS and TBT Measures of Bhutan (4)	Details of SPS and TBT Agency of Bhutan (5)	SPS and TBT Measures of Bangladesh (6)	Details of SPS and TBT Agency of Bangladesh (7)	Details of Procedural Obstacles in Bhutan (8)	Details of Procedural Obstacles in Bangladesh (9)
40	470790	Waste and scrap of paper or paperboard, NES (including unsorted waste and scrap)	No TBT measures identified	BSB	B19: Prohibitions or restrictions of imports for objectives set out in the TBT agreement (importable for use as industrial raw material)	Import Policy Order, 2012–2015 Ministry of Commerce	Not known	Not known
41	721320	Hot-rolled bars and rods, including non-alloy steel, hot-rolled, in irregular wound coils, of free-cutting steel	A83: Certification B14: Authorization requirement for TBT reasons, labeling requirements	BSB DOT, MOEA Sales Tax, Customs and Excise Act, 2000	B19: Prohibitions or restrictions of imports for objectives set out in the TBT agreement; only recognized bona fide user industrial unit shall be allowed to import iron and steel waste and scrap	Import Policy Order, 2012–2015 Ministry of Commerce		
42	800200	Tin waste and scrap	No TBT measures identified	BSB	E329: Prohibition for noneconomic reason NES Not importable	Import Policy Order, 2012–2015 Ministry of Commerce		Sold by informal scrap dealers across to Indian border towns; presumably bought by recycling middlemen
43	940360	Furniture, wooden, NES	No TBT measures identified	BSB DOT, MOEA	No TBT measures identified	Import Policy Order, 2012–2015 Ministry of Commerce National Board of Revenue	Lack of reliable dealership in Bangladesh	Banking transactions delays based on current exports Longer distance to markets as compared to markets in border towns of India
44	150790	Soybean oil and its fractions, refined but not chemically modified	A83: Certification requirements	BAFRA BSB	A83: Certification requirement (imports subject to submission of a certificate from BSTI); crude soybean oil up to the quantity limit (as determined by the sponsoring authority) will be importable for use in production of edible oil by recognized edible oil-producing industrial units	Import Policy Order, 2012–2015 Ministry of Commerce		Banking transactions delays based on current exports Longer distance to markets as compared to markets in border towns of India

continued on next page

Table A3.1 continued

Series No. (1)	HS Code (2)	Description (3)	SPS and TBT Measures of Bhutan (4)	Details of SPS and TBT Agency of Bhutan (5)	SPS and TBT Measures of Bangladesh (6)	Details of SPS and TBT Agency of Bangladesh (7)	Details of Procedural Obstacles in Bhutan (8)	Details of Procedural Obstacles in Bangladesh (9)
45	550912	Yarn containing greater than or equal to 85% nylon or other polyamide staple fibers, multi, not put up, NES	SPS and TBT measures in Bhutan not identified. Standards on natural dye under study	BAFRA BSB	No TBT and SPS measures identified	Import Policy Order, 2012–2015. Ministry of Commerce. National Board of Revenue	Not known	Not known
46	540234	Textured synthetic filament yarn of polypropylene (excluding sewing thread)	SPS and TBT measures in Bhutan not identified	BAFRA BSB	No TBT and SPS measures identified	Import Policy Order, 2012–2015. Ministry of Commerce. National Board of Revenue	Not known	Not known
47	220830	Whiskies	E121: Special authorization requirements for religious, cultural, and moral reasons	BAFRA DOT, MOEA MOF Sales Tax, Customs and Excise Act, 2000	E321: Prohibition for religious, moral, or cultural reasons. G332: Importers' own foreign exchange	Import Policy Order, 2012–2015; VAT Act, 1991; and Customs Act, 1969. Ministry of Commerce	Not known	Not known
48	271320	Petroleum bitumen in drum	B14: Authorization requirements for TBT reasons. E111: Licensing procedure with no specific ex ante criteria. BTS IS 3117, BTS IS 8887	BAFRA. BSB. DOT, MOEA	E311 Full prohibition (import ban)	Import Policy Order, 2012–2015. Ministry of Commerce. National Board of Revenue	Not known	Banking transactions delays based on current exports. Longer distance to markets as compared to markets in border towns of India
49	070610	Carrots, turnips	A83: Certification requirements. A14: Special authorization requirement for SPS reasons	BAFRA		Import Policy Order, 2012–2015. Ministry of Commerce. National Board of Revenue	High risk on product perishability with long distance to markets and lengthy border customs procedures	Long distance to markets, perishability

continued on next page

Table A3.1 continued

Series No. (1)	HS Code (2)	Description (3)	SPS and TBT Measures of Bhutan (4)	Details of SPS and TBT Agency of Bhutan (5)	SPS and TBT Measures of Bangladesh (6)	Details of SPS and TBT Agency of Bangladesh (7)	Details of Procedural Obstacles in Bhutan (8)	Details of Procedural Obstacles in Bangladesh (9)
50	392329	Sacks and bags (including cones) of plastics NES	SPS and TBT measures in Bhutan not identified	BAFRA BSB DOT, MOEA	No SPS and TBT measures identified	National Board of Revenue	Lengthy border customs formalities	Lengthy border customs formalities
51	392350	Stoppers, lids, caps, and other closures of plastics	SPS and TBT measures in Bhutan not identified	BAFRA BSB		Import Policy Order, 2012–2015	Not known	Not known
52	200919	Orange juice and NES, unfermented and not spirited, whether or not sugared or sweet	A83: Certification requirements	BAFRA Sales Tax, Customs and Excise Act, 2000		Ministry of Commerce National Board of Revenue	Long transport distance to border of Bangladesh Transshipment and banking delays	Banking transactions delays based on current exports Longer distance to markets as compared to markets in border towns of India
53	540233	Textured yarn NES, of polyester filaments, not put up for retail sale	SPS and TBT measures in Bhutan not identified	BAFRA BSB	SPS and TBT measures in Bangladesh not identified	Import Policy Order, 2012–2015	Long transport distance to border of Bangladesh Transshipment and banking delays	Banking transactions delays based on current exports

BAFRA = Bhutan Agriculture and Food Regulatory Authority, BDS = Bangladesh Standards, BSB = Bhutan Standards Bureau, BSTI = Bangladesh Standards and Testing Institution, BTS = Bureau of Transportation Statistics, DOT = Department of Trade, GST = goods and services tax, HS = Harmonized System, IS = Indian standard, MOEA = Ministry of Economic Affairs, MOF = Ministry of Finance, NES = not elsewhere specified, OPC = ordinary Portland cement, SARSO = South Asian Regional Standards Organization, SPS = sanitary and phytosanitary, TBT = technical barrier to trade, VAT = value-added tax.

Sources: Government of Bhutan, MOF, Department of Revenue and Customs. 2016. *Bhutan Trade Statistics 2015*. Thimphu; S. Raihan, M.A. Khan, and S. Quoreshi. 2014. *NTMs in South Asia: Assessment and Analysis*. Kathmandu: South Asian Association for Regional Cooperation Trade Promotion Network; Government of Bangladesh, Bangladesh Customs. *Harmonised Tariff of Bangladesh Customs*; Government of Bangladesh, *Bangladesh Customs. Bangladesh Customs National Tariff: Fiscal Year 2016–2017*; and United Nations. United Nations Comtrade Database (accessed August 2017).

Table A3.2: Existing Gaps in Indian Market

Series No. (1)	HS Code (2)	Description (3)	SPS and TBT Measures of Bhutan (4)	Details of SPS and TBT Agency of Bhutan (5)	SPS and TBT Measures of India (6)	Details of SPS and TBT Agency of India (7)	Details of Procedural obstacles in Bhutan (8)	Details of Procedural Obstacles in India (9)
1	08	Oranges, fresh (080510) Apples, fresh (080810)	BAFRA food safety certification, fit for consumption Proper grading, packaging, and labeling, country of origin certificate Draft standards under preparation by SARSO with Bhutan as lead, also including potato	BAFRA DRC MOF	Consignments are packed in such a manner that it facilitates inspection and collection of samples Requires country of export certification 19 requirements, including packaging, labeling, food additives, storage, contaminants, and toxins	Food Safety and Standards (Food Import) Regulations, 2016 General Grading and Marking Rules, 1998	Documentation time lags, customs gate closure timings Road strikes across border towns, transshipment at Changrabandha and Burimari toll gates	Border customs delays in documentation Imports are subject to marking, certification, inspection, and testing requirements Time delays Road strikes across border towns, transshipment at Changrabandha and Burimari toll gates
2	09	Cardamoms (090831) Pepper, neither crushed nor ground (090411)	BAFRA inspection and export certification BAFRA certification on food safety No national standards identified	BAFRA BSB	Food safety certification by border customs authority from reputed institutions in Kolkata, India Consignments must be packed in such a manner that it facilitates inspection and collection of samples Any imported food article shall be sent to laboratories notified by FSSAI 22 requirements, including packaging, labeling, marking, grading, additives, GMOs, toxins, and contaminants	FSSAI Food Safety and Standards Regulations, 2011	High transaction cost with scattered production sites makes collection and assembly difficult Long transportation distance between farms and export points Limited auction infrastructure, roadblocks during monsoons	Indian border customs requires a fit for human consumption certificate (with testing conducted in a renowned lab in India) in addition to a phytosanitary certificate issued by BAFRA Every consignment is checked for certification Exports facilitated by Indian traders participating in auctions and arranging their own transport

continued on next page

Table A3.2 continued

Series No. (1)	HS Code (2)	Description (3)	SPS and TBT Measures of Bhutan (4)	Details of SPS and TBT Agency of Bhutan (5)	SPS and TBT Measures of India (6)	Details of SPS and TBT Agency of India (7)	Details of Procedural obstacles in Bhutan (8)	Details of Procedural Obstacles in India (9)
3	270112	Bituminous coal, whether or not pulverized, but not agglomerated	B14: Authorization requirements for TBT reasons E111: Licensing procedures with no specific ex ante criteria	BSB	All packaged commodities must bear a label with the name and address of the manufacturer or importer, net quantity, and the date packed Commodities must be packed in standard quantities by weight, measure, or number. 2 for labeling and packaging	CBEC	Transportation dependent on Indian truckers plying in Indian highways subject road strikes, transport service charge of 5% extra levied by local authorities	18% GST No issue but requires good personal relation with local authorities
4	25	Natural steatite, crushed or powdered (252620) Natural steatite, not crushed or powdered (252610) Pebbles, gravel, broken or crushed stone used for aggregates, (251710) Mineral substances, NES (253090)	No TBT measures identified	Requires Department of Forests and Park Services clearance Requires DRC export license	Legal Metrology (Packaged Commodities) Rules, 2011 All packaged commodities must bear a label with the name and address of the manufacturer or importer, net quantity, and the date packed Commodities must be packed in standard quantities by weight, measure, or number 3 requirements, including plant quarantine, import regulations, and special authorizations	CBEC.	Forest protection clearance delays and road strikes.	Border customs delays in documentation. Imports are subject to marking, certification, inspection and testing requirements. Time delays.

continued on next page

Table A3.2 continued

Series No. (1)	HS Code (2)	Description (3)	SPS and TBT Measures of Bhutan (4)	Details of SPS and TBT Agency of Bhutan (5)	SPS and TBT Measures of India (6)	Details of SPS and TBT Agency of India (7)	Details of Procedural obstacles in Bhutan (8)	Details of Procedural Obstacles in India (9)
5	283650	Calcium Carbonate	No identified TBT measures.	DRC Export License.	Meets Bureau of Indian Standards as per IS 1559-1961 3 requirements on labeling, packaging, and registration	CBEC	Delays at border customs office with inadequate customs infrastructure	18% GST, Government of Bhutan slow to respond to such developments in India
6	270400	Coke and semicoke of coal, lignite, or peat; agglomerated or not, retort carbon	B14: Authorization requirements for TBT reasons E111: Licensing procedures with no specific ex ante criteria	BAFRA DRC export license	Antidumping Customs Tariff Act, 1975 Customs Tariff (Identification, Assessment & Collection of Anti-Dumping Duty on Dumped Articles and for Determination of Injury) Rules, 1995 3 requirements, including plant quarantine, import regulations, and special authorizations	CBEC	Lengthy formalities with Bhutan customs and trade licensing authorities	Border customs delays in documentation Imports are subject to marking, certification, inspection. and testing requirements Time delays
7	20	Fruit and vegetable juice NES (excluding mix) unfermented, unspirited, whether or not sugared or sweet (200980) Vegetables and mixtures of vegetables, prepared or preserved (200599) Vegetables and mixtures of vegetables, prepared (200599)	B14: Authorization requirements for TBT reasons A83: Certification and inspection requirements	BAFRA Food Corporation of Bhutan auction	All products need to be tested and certified by an accredited lab in Kolkata, India. BAFRA Rules of Origin Value addition certificate, FSSAI 15 requirements, including packaging, labeling, grading, residues, import controls, sample analysis, and additives	FSSAI.	Limited auction infrastructure, roadblocks during monsoons	It takes a minimum of 10 days for test results to arrive No imports on milk since 2013

continued on next page

Appendix 3   77

Table A3.2 continued

Series No. (1)	HS Code (2)	Description (3)	SPS and TBT Measures of Bhutan (4)	Details of SPS and TBT Agency of Bhutan (5)	SPS and TBT Measures of India (6)	Details of SPS and TBT Agency of India (7)	Details of Procedural obstacles in Bhutan (8)	Details of Procedural Obstacles in India (9)
8	10	Rice, semi-milled or wholly milled, whether or not polished or glazed (100630)	A83 certification and inspection requirements	BAFRA certification DRC export license	Requires 21 regulations, including packaging, labeling, FSSAI, marking and grading rules, import policy, additives, radiation processing, and plant quarantine		High transaction cost and high per-unit cost because of low volume	None

BAFRA = Bhutan Agriculture and Food Regulatory Authority, BSB = Bhutan Standards Bureau, CBEC = Central Board of Excise and Customs, DRC = Department of Revenue and Customs, FSSAI = Food Safety and Standards Authority of India, GMO = genetically modified organism, GST = goods and services tax, HS = Harmonized System, IS = Indian standard, MOF = Ministry of Finance, NES = not elsewhere specified, SARSO = South Asian Regional Standards Organization, SPS = sanitary and phytosanitary, TBT = technical barrier to trade.

Sources: International Trade Centre. Market Access Map; Government of Bhutan, MOF, DRC. 2016. *Bhutan Trade Statistics 2015*. Thimphu; and United Nations. United Nations Comtrade database (accessed August 2017).

Table A3.3: Existing Gaps in Nepal Market

Series No. (1)	HS Code (2)	Description (3)	SPS and TBT Measures of Bhutan (4)	Details of SPS and TBT Agency of Bhutan (5)	SPS and TBT Measures of Nepal (6)	Details of SPS and TBT Agency of Nepal (7)	Details of Procedural Obstacles in Bhutan (8)	Details of Procedural Obstacles in Nepal (9)
1	72	Ferrosilicon (720221) Semifinished product, iron, and non-alloy steel (720712) Waste scrap cast iron (720410) Semifinished product, iron, or non-alloy steel (720719) Ferro-silico-manganese (720230) Bars and rods (722860)	No TBT measures identified	BSB DOT, MOEA DRC, MOF	B1: Prohibitions or restrictions of imports for objectives set out in the TBT agreement B7: Product quality or performance requirement B83: certification requirement 9 requirements, including conformity assessments, regulation of foreign exchange, terms of payment, and import authorization	NBSM's regulation in accordance with Nepal Standards Certification Mark Act, 1980 (2037)	Regular documentation for exports like invoicing, trans-shipment at border customs of India and Nepal	Not known

continued on next page

Table A3.3 continued

Series No. (1)	HS Code (2)	Description (3)	SPS and TBT Measures of Bhutan (4)	Details of SPS and TBT Agency of Bhutan (5)	SPS and TBT Measures of Nepal (6)	Details of SPS and TBT Agency of Nepal (7)	Details of Procedural Obstacles in Bhutan (8)	Details of Procedural Obstacles in Nepal (9)
2	25	Portland cement (252329) Dolomite (251810) Limestone and other calcareous stone or cement (252100) Cement clinkers (252310) Gypsum (252010) Plasters consisting of calcined gypsum or calcium sulfate (252020) Natural steatite, crushed or powdered (252620) Quicklime (252210) Quartzite (250620) Natural steatite (252610)	No TBT measures identified	BSB DOT, MOEA DRC, MOF	B7: Product quality or performance requirement A21: Tolerance limits for residues of or contamination by certain (non-microbiological) substances B83: Certification requirements B14: Authorization requirement for TBT reasons 14 requirements, including marking, packing and product identifying, tolerance limits, and other banking regulations	NBSM's regulation in accordance with Nepal Standards Certification Mark Act, 1980 (2037) DFTQC, Ministry of Agricultural Development	Not known	Not known
3	28	Calcium carbide (284910) Silicon (280469, 281122) Calcium carbonate (283650) Carbides (284990) Oxygen (280440)	No TBT measures identified	BSB DOT, MOEA DRC, MOF	B14: Authorization requirement for TBT reasons 9 requirements in total	Ministry of Commerce	Regular documentation for exports like invoicing, trans-shipment at border customs of India and Nepal	Not known
4	74	Wire of refined copper (740819) Waste scrap copper (74040) Billets copper (740313) Waste and scrap, copper, or copper alloy (740400)	No TBT measures identified	BSB DOT, MOEA DRC, MOF	B7: Product quality or performance requirement B83: Certification requirement In total 11 requirements	NBSM's regulation in accordance with Nepal Standards Certification Mark Act, 1980 (2037) NBSM, Ministry of Industry	Not known	Not known

continued on next page

Table A3.3 continued

Series No. (1)	HS Code (2)	Description (3)	SPS and TBT Measures of Bhutan (4)	Details of SPS and TBT Agency of Bhutan (5)	SPS and TBT Measures of Nepal (6)	Details of SPS and TBT Agency of Nepal (7)	Details of Procedural Obstacles in Bhutan (8)	Details of Procedural Obstacles in Nepal (9)
5	08	Oranges, fresh (080510) Apples, fresh (080810) Edible nuts (080290)	A83: Certification and inspection requirements	BAFRA Food Corporation of Bhutan DOT, MOEA DRC, MOF	A14: Special authorization requirements for SPS reasons A83: Certification requirements In total 10 requirements	Plant Protection Rules, 2010 Plant Protection Act, 2007 Ministry of Agriculture and Cooperatives, Department of Agriculture Plant Protection Directorate National Plant Protection Program	High transaction cost stemming from assembly to achieve economies of scale, documentation, and BAFRA certification	Long distance on road Payment delays
6	07	Potatoes, fresh (070190, 71010) Lentils, dried and shelled (071340)	A14: Special authorization requirements for SPS reasons A83: Certification requirements	BAFRA Food Corporation of Bhutan DOT, MOEA	A14: Special authorization requirements for SPS reasons B14: Authorization requirement for TBT reasons A21: Tolerance limits for residues of or contamination by certain (non-microbiological) substances A22: Restricted use of certain substances in foods and feeds and their contact materials B31: Labeling requirements In total 11 requirements	Food Act, 2013 Food Rules, Seed Act	Not known	Export license requirements
7	39	Film and sheet, (392099) Fittings, plastic (391740)	B14: Authorization requirement for TBT reasons	BSB DOT, MOEA DRC, MOF	B14: Authorization requirement for TBT reasons In total 11 requirements	Ministry of Commerce	Not known	Not known

continued on next page

Table A3.3 continued

Series No. (1)	HS Code (2)	Description (3)	SPS and TBT Measures of Bhutan (4)	Details of SPS and TBT Agency of Bhutan (5)	SPS and TBT Measures of Nepal (6)	Details of SPS and TBT Agency of Nepal (7)	Details of Procedural Obstacles in Bhutan (8)	Details of Procedural Obstacles in Nepal (9)
		Sacks and bags (392321, 392329) Tubes, pipes, and hoses (391729) Tube, hoses (391731)	E111: Licensing procedures with no specific ex ante criteria					
8	22	Undenatured ethyl alcohol (220710) Beer (220300) Rum and tafia (220840) Whiskies (220830) Ethyl alcohol (220720), Undenatured ethyl alcohol (220890) Mineral and aerated waters (220110) Vinegar and substitutes (220900)	E121: Special authorization requirements for cultural or moral reasons	BSB DOT, MOEA DRC, MOF	A14: Special authorization requirements for SPS reasons B14: Authorization requirement for TBT reasons A21: Tolerance limits for residues of or contamination by certain (non-microbiological) substances A22: Restricted use of certain substances in foods and feeds and their contact materials A31, B31: Labeling requirements In total 10 requirements	DFTQC, Ministry of Agricultural Development	Not known	Not known
9	11	Wheat or meslin flour (110100) Wheat groats (110311)	A83: Certification and inspection requirements	BSB DOT, MOEA DRC, MOF	A14: Special authorization requirements for SPS reasons A21: Tolerance limits for residues of or contamination by certain (non-microbiological) substances A22: Restricted use of certain substances in foods and feeds and their contact materials	DFTQC, Ministry of Agricultural Development	Not known	Not known

continued on next page

Table A3.3 continued

Series No. (1)	HS Code (2)	Description (3)	SPS and TBT Measures of Bhutan (4)	Details of SPS and TBT Agency of Bhutan (5)	SPS and TBT Measures of Nepal (6)	Details of SPS and TBT Agency of Nepal (7)	Details of Procedural Obstacles in Bhutan (8)	Details of Procedural Obstacles in Nepal (9)
					A31, B31: Labeling requirements In total 10 requirements			
10	20	Juice of fruit or vegetables (200989) Homogenized preparations (200710) Orange juice (200911, 200919) Apple juice, unfermented (200971) Citrus fruit processed (200791) Citrus fruit juice (200931)	A83: Certification and inspection requirements	BSB DOT, MOEA DRC, MOF	A14: Special authorization requirements for SPS reasons A21: Tolerance limits for residues of or contamination by certain (non-microbiological) substances A22: Restricted use of certain substances in foods and feeds and their contact materials A31, B31: Labeling requirements In total 10 requirements	DFTQC, Ministry of Agricultural Development	Not known	Not known
11	21	Protein concentrates and textured protein substances (210610) Tomato ketchup (210320)	A83: Certification and inspection requirements	BSB DOT, MOEA DRC, MOF	A14: Special authorization requirements for SPS reasons A21: Tolerance limits for residues of or contamination by certain (non-microbiological) substances A22: Restricted use of certain substances in foods and feeds and their contact materials A31, B31: Labeling requirements In total 10 requirements	DFTQC, Ministry of Agricultural Development	Not known	Not known

continued on next page

Table A3.3 continued

Series No. (1)	HS Code (2)	Description (3)	SPS and TBT Measures of Bhutan (4)	Details of SPS and TBT Agency of Bhutan (5)	SPS and TBT Measures of Nepal (6)	Details of SPS and TBT Agency of Nepal (7)	Details of Procedural Obstacles in Bhutan (8)	Details of Procedural Obstacles in Nepal (9)
12	44	Wood charcoal, including shell or nut charcoal, whether or not agglomerate (440290) Plywood (441231) Veneered panels (441294) Plywood of sheets of wood (441232) Doors and frames of wood (441820)	No SPS and TBT measures identified	No SPS and TBT measures identified	Conformity assessments, authorization of TBT requirements, banking regulations In total 10 requirements	No SPS and TBT measures identified	Not known	Not known
13	09	Ginger: Neither crushed nor ground (091011) Spices (091099)	A83: Certification and inspection requirements	BAFRA Food Corporation of Bhutan DOT, MOEA	A22: Restricted use of certain substances in foods and feeds and their contact materials A21: Tolerance limits for residues of or contamination by certain (non-microbiological) substances In total 10 requirements	Ministry of Agriculture and Cooperatives, Department of Agriculture Plant Protection Directorate National Plant Quarantine Program	Not known	Not known
14	26	Slag, dross (261900) Granulated slag (261800)	No TBT and SPS measures identified	No TBT and SPS measures identified	No TBT and SPS measures identified	No TBT and SPS measures identified	Not known	Not known
15	70	Carboys, bottles, flasks (701090)	No TBT and SPS measures identified	No TBT and SPS measures identified	No TBT and SPS measures identified	No TBT and SPS measures identified	Not known	Not known
16	47	Waste and scrap of paper or paperboard (470790)	No TBT and SPS measures identified	No TBT and SPS measures identified	No TBT and SPS measures identified	No TBT and SPS measures identified	Not known	Not known
17	80	Tin waste and scrap (800200)	No TBT and SPS measures identified	No TBT and SPS measures identified	No TBT and SPS measures identified	No TBT and SPS measures identified	Not known	Not known
18	94	Furniture, wooden (940360) Bedroom furniture (940350)	No TBT and SPS measures identified	BSB standards and certification	No TBT and SPS measures identified	No TBT and SPS measures identified	Not known	Not known

continued on next page

Appendix 3　83

Table A3.3 continued

Series No. (1)	HS Code (2)	Description (3)	SPS and TBT Measures of Bhutan (4)	Details of SPS and TBT Agency of Bhutan (5)	SPS and TBT Measures of Nepal (6)	Details of SPS and TBT Agency of Nepal (7)	Details of Procedural Obstacles in Bhutan (8)	Details of Procedural Obstacles in Nepal (9)
19	15	Soybean oil and its fractions (150790)	A83: Certification	BSB DOT, MOEA DRC, MOF	A22: Restricted use of certain substances in foods and feeds and their contact materials; TBT regulations on production processes In total 13 requirements	Ministry of Agriculture and Cooperatives, Department of Agriculture Plant Protection Directorate National Plant Quarantine Program	Not known	Not known
20	54	Textured synthetic filament yarn of polypropylene (540234)	No TBT and SPS measures identified	BSB	No SPS and TBT measures known		Not known	Not known
21	27	Petroleum bitumen (271320)	No TBT and SPS measures identified	DOT, MOEA	Only state trading companies can import, internal taxes and charges, testing requirements In total 13 requirements		Not known	Not known
22	54	Textured yarn (540233)	No TBT and SPS measures identified	No TBT and SPS measures identified	No SPS and TBT measures identified		Not known	Not known
23	76	Waste and scrap, aluminum (760200)	No TBT and SPS measures identified	No TBT and SPS measures identified	B14: Authorization requirement for TBT reasons Mandatory 10 requirements	Ministry of Commerce	Not known	Not known
24	34	Soap and original surfactant preparation (340119)	No TBT and SPS measures identified	No TBT and SPS measures identified	B14: Authorization requirement for TBT reasons Mandatory 10 requirements		Not known	Not known
25	04	Milk, not concentrated and unsweetened (040120)	A83: Certification and inspection requirements	BAFRA standards, food safety certification	A14: Special authorization requirements for SPS reasons B14: Authorization requirement for TBT reasons A21: Tolerance limits for residues of or contamination by certain (non-microbiological) substances	DFTQC, Ministry of Agricultural Development	Dependent on Indian roads and political stability	Payment delays

continued on next page

Table A3.3 continued

Series No. (1)	HS Code (2)	Description (3)	SPS and TBT Measures of Bhutan (4)	Details of SPS and TBT Agency of Bhutan (5)	SPS and TBT Measures of Nepal (6)	Details of SPS and TBT Agency of Nepal (7)	Details of Procedural Obstacles in Bhutan (8)	Details of Procedural Obstacles in Nepal (9)
					A22: Restricted use of certain substances in foods and feeds and their contact materials In total 10 requirements			
26	23	Animal feed preparations (230990)	A83: Certification and inspection requirements	BAFRA standards, animal safety certification	A21: Tolerance limits for residues of or contamination by certain (non-microbiological) substances A14: Special authorization requirements for SPS reasons B14: Authorization requirement for TBT reasons In total 15 requirements	DFTQC, Ministry of Agricultural Development	Not known	Not known

BAFRA = Bhutan Agriculture and Food Regulatory Authority, BSB = Bhutan Standards Bureau, DFTQC = Department of Food Technology and Quality Control, DOT = Department of Trade, DRC = Department of Revenue and Customs, HS = Harmonized System, MOEA = Ministry of Economic Affairs, MOF = Ministry of Finance, NBSM = Nepal Bureau of Standards and Metrology, SPS = sanitary and phytosanitary, TBT = technical barrier to trade.

Sources: International Trade Centre. Market Access Map; Government of Bhutan, MOF, DRC. 2016. *Bhutan Trade Statistics 2015*. Thimphu; and United Nations. United Nations Comtrade database (accessed August 2017).

Appendix 4
Products for Exemption of Customs Duty

Table A4.1: Exportable Products from Bhutan to Bangladesh

Series No.	HS Code	Description of Goods
1	0403.10	Yogurt
2	0406.10–0406.90	Cheese and curd
3	0409.00	Natural honey
4	0701.90	Potatoes
5	0704.10	Cauliflowers and headed broccoli
6	0704.20	Brussels sprouts
7	0704.90	Edible Brassicas (cabbages, kohlrabi, kale, Etc.), Others, Fresh Or Chilled
8	0706.10	Carrots and turnips
9	0706.90	Salad Beets (salad beetroot), Salsify, Celeriac, Radishes And Edible Roots
10	0708.10–0708.90	Leguminous vegetables, shelled or unshelled, fresh or chilled
11	0709.20	Asparagus
12	0709.51	Mushrooms of the genus *Agaricus*
13	0709.60	Chilies, fresh
14	0712.31	Mushrooms and truffles, dried
15	0713.33	Kidney beans, including white pea beans (*Phaseolus vulgaris*)
16	0802.31	In shell (walnut)
17	0805.10	Oranges
18	0805.20	Mandarins
19	0808.10	Apples
20	0808.30–0808.40	Pears and quinces
21	0809.10	Apricots
22	0809.30	Peaches, including nectarines
23	0809.40	Plums and sloes, fresh
24	0810.10–0810.90	Other fruit, fresh (strawberries and persimmon)
25	0813.40	Other fruit (dried persimmon)
26	0814.00	Peel of citrus fruit or melons (including watermelons), fresh, frozen, dried, or provisionally preserved in brine, in sulfur water, or in other preservative solutions.
27	0904.22	Fruits of the genus *Capsicum* or of the genus *Pimenta*, dried or crushed or ground
28	0908.30–0908.32	Cardamoms

continued on next page

Table A4.1 continued

Series No.	HS Code	Description of Goods
29	1005.10–1005.90	Maize
30	1006.20.00	Husked brown rice
31	0910.10–0910.12	Ginger
32	1511.10–1511.90	Palm oil and its fractions, whether or not refined but not chemically modified
33	1517.10–1517.90	Margarine, edible mixtures or preparations of animal or vegetable fat or oils, or fractions of different fats or oils of this chapter, other than edible fats or oils or their fractions of heading no. 15.16
34	2001.90	Other (pickles)
35	2002.10	Tomatoes, whole or in pieces
36	2003.10	Mushrooms of the genus *Agaricus*
37	2005.10	Homogenized vegetables
38	2005.60	Asparagus
39	2005.80	Sweet corn (*Zea mays* var. saccharata)
40	2005.91–2005.99	Other vegetables and mixtures of vegetables, prepared or preserved
41	2006.00	Vegetables, fruit, nuts, fruit-peel and other parts of plants, preserved by sugar (drained, glace, or crystallized)
42	2007.10–2007.99	Homogenized preparation of jams, fruit jellies, marmalades, fruit or nut puree, and fruit or nut pastes, being cooked preparations, whether or not containing added sugar or other sweetening matter
43	2008.11.00	Groundnuts
44	2008.19.00	Others, including mixtures
45	2008.20.00	Pineapples
46	2008.30.00	Citrus fruit
47	2008.40.00	Pears
48	2008.50.00	Apricots
49	2008.60.00	Cherries
50	2008.70.00	Peaches, including nectarines
51	2008.91.00	Palm hearts
52	2009.11.00	Orange juice; Frozen
53	2009.12.00	Not frozen, of a Brix value not exceeding 20
54	2009.19.00	Other juice
55	2009.29–2009.89	Fruit juices (including grape must) and vegetable juices, unfermented and not containing added spirits, whether or not containing added sugar or other sweetening matter
56	2009.90	Mixtures of juices
57	2103.20	Tomato ketchup and other tomato sauces
58	2201.10	Mineral waters and aerated waters
59	2202.10	Waters, including mineral waters and aerated waters, containing added sugar or other sweetening matter or flavored

continued on next page

Table A4.1 continued

Series No.	HS Code	Description of Goods
60	2506.10–2506.20	Quartz (other than natural sands); quartzite, whether or not roughly trimmed or merely cut, by sawing or otherwise, into blocks or slabs or a rectangular (including square) shape
61	2515.11–2515.12	Marble, travertine, ecaussine, and other calcareous monumental and building stone of an apparent specific gravity of 2.5 or more, and alabaster, whether or not roughly trimmed or merely cut, by sawing or otherwise, into blocks or slabs of a rectangular (including square) shape
62	2515.12	Merely cut, by sawing or otherwise, into blocks or slabs of a rectangular (including square) shape
63	2516.11–2516.90	Granite, porphyry, basalt, sandstone and other monumental or building stone, whether or not roughly trimmed or merely cut, by sawing or otherwise, into blocks or slabs of a rectangular (including square) shape
64	2517.10.00	Pebbles, gravel, broken or crushed stone, of a kind commonly used for concrete aggregates, for road metaling, or for railway or other ballast, shingle and flint, whether or not heat-treated
65	2517.41.00	Granules, chippings, powder of marble
66	2518.10–2518.30	Dolomite, whether or not calcined; dolomite roughly trimmed or merely cut, by sawing or otherwise, into blocks or slabs of a rectangular (including square) shape; agglomerated dolomite (including tarred dolomite)
67	2520.10.00	Gypsum; anhydrite
68	2520.20.00	Plasters
69	2521.00.00	Limestone flux; limestone and other calcareous stone, of a kind used for the manufacture of lime or cement
70	2522.10–2522.30	Quicklime, slaked lime, and hydraulic lime, other than calcium oxide and hydroxide of heading no. 28.25
71	2523.10.00	Cement clinkers
72	2523.21–2523.29	Portland cement
73	2526.10–2526.20	Natural steatite, whether or not roughly trimmed or merely cut, by sawing or otherwise into blocks or slabs of a rectangular (including square) shape; talc
74	2701.11–2701.19	Coal
75	2849.10–2849.90	Carbides, whether or not chemically defined
76	3301.29.00	Other (essential oils)
77	3806.10	Gum resin
78	3917.21–3917.40	Tubes, pipes, and hoses, rigid (HDPE pipes)
79	4410.11–4410.90	Particle board, oriented strand board, and similar board (for example, waferboard) of wood or other ligneous materials, whether or not agglomerated with resins or other organic binding substances
80	4411.12–4411.94	Fiber board of wood or other ligneous materials, whether or not bonded with resins or other organic substances
81	4412.10–4412.99	Plywood, veneered panels, and similar laminated wood
82	4418.10–4418.90	Builders' joinery and carpentry of wood, including cellular wood panels, assembled flooring panels, shingles, and shakes

continued on next page

Table A4.1 continued

Series No.	HS Code	Description of Goods
83	5402.33–5402.47	Textured polyester yarn
84	7202.21–7202.29	Ferrosilicon
85	7206.10–7206.90	Iron and non-alloy steel in ingots or other primary forms (excluding iron of heading no. 72.03)
86	7207.11–7207.20	Semifinished products of iron or non-alloy steel
87	7216.10–7216.99	Angles, shapes, and sections of iron or non-alloy steel
88	7222.11–7222.40	Bars and rods, not further worked than hot-rolled, hot-drawn, or extruded
89	7408.11–7408.19	Copper wire
90	9403.30–9403.90	Furniture

HDPE = high-density polyethylene, HS = Harmonized System.

Source: Government of Bhutan and Government of India. 2016. *Agreement on Trade, Commerce and Transit between the Royal Government of Bhutan and the Government of the Republic of India.* Thimphu.

Table A4.2: Exportable Products from Bangladesh to Bhutan

Series No.	HS Code	Description of Goods
1	0305.59	Dried fish, whether or not salted, but not smoked
2	0402.99	Condensed milk
3	0701.90	Potatoes, fresh or chilled
4	0902.30	Black tea (packed)
5	1704.90	Other sugar confectionary (candy)
6	1905.10–1905.90	Bread and biscuits
7	2009.31	Juice of any other single fruit: other
8	2009.89	Juice of any other single fruit or vegetable: other
9	2104.20	Homogenized composite food preparations
10	2523.29	Cement
11	2710.19	Other: petroleum oils obtained from bituminous material
12	3003.10–3006.92	Pharmaceutical goods
13	3304.91	Powders, whether or not compressed
14	3304.99	Other beauty, makeup, skin care preparations
15	3305.10	Shampoos
16	3305.90	Hair dyes and oil and tonic
17	3306.10	Dentifrices
18	3307.10–3307.90	Cosmetics
19	3401.11–3401.20	Soap (toilet use)
20	3401.19	Soap (ordinary)
21	3917.23	Tubes, pipes, and hoses of polymers of vinyl chloride
22	3919.90	Other plastic goods and sheets
23	3921.90	Plastic strips, other

continued on next page

Table A4.2 continued

Series No.	HS Code	Description of Goods
24	3923.10	Boxes, cases, crates, and similar articles of plastic
25	3923.21	Sacks and bags (including cones) of polymers of ethylene
26	3923.20	Sacks and bags (including cones) of other plastic
27	3924.10	Tableware and kitchenware of plastics
28	4202.11	Trunks, suitcase, briefcase of leather
29	4911.10	Trade advertising material, commercial catalogs and the like
30	5310.10	Unbleached fabrics of jute
31	5310.90	Other fabrics of jute
32	5607.10	Twine, cordage, ropes, and cables of jute
33	5702.20	Jute or coconut fibers carpets
34	5703.90	Jute carpet and other textile floor coverings
35	6103.32	Jacket and blazers of cotton
36	6109.10	T-shirts, singlets, and other vests knitted or crocheted of cotton
37	6109.90	T-shirts, singlets, and other vests knitted or crocheted of other textile materials
38	6117.10	Hosiery goods, shawls, scarves, mufflers, veils
39	6201.99	Overcoats, wind jackets of other textile materials
40	6203.32	Jacket and blazers of cotton
41	6205.10	Men's or boys' shirts of wool and fine animal hair
42	6205.20	Men's or boys' shirts of cotton
43	6205.30	Men's or boys' shirts of synthetic fiber
44	6205.90	Men's or boys' shirts of other textile materials
45	6208.11	Women's or girls' slip and petticoats of synthetic fiber
46	6208.21	Women's or girls' nightdresses and pajamas of cotton
47	6211.31	Garments for males, of wool
48	6211.41	Garments for females, of wool
49	6303.29	Bed sheets, bed linen, of other materials
50	6305.10	Sacks and bags of a kind used for the packing of jute
51	6403.20	Footwear with outer soles of leather, and uppers consisting of leather straps across the instep and around the big toe
52	6404.20	Footwear with outer soles of leather or composition leather
53	6405.90	Other footwear (sandals, slippers)
54	6505.90	Other hats and headgear
55	6902.10–6902.90	Ceramic tiles
56	6911.10	Tableware and kitchenware of porcelain or china
57	7210.41	Corrugated iron sheets
58	7214.10–7214.60	Iron rods
59	7408.11–7408.19	Copper wire
60	7610.10	Aluminum doors and windows

continued on next page

Table A4.2 continued

Series No.	HS Code	Description of Goods
61	8212.20	Safety razor blades, including razor blades in strips
62	8414.51	Fans: table, floor, wall, ceiling
63	8504.21–8504.40	Electrical transformer and static converters
64	8506.10	Dry cell battery
65	8507.10	Lead-acid, of a kind used for starting piston engines
66	8539.22	Other filament lamp of a power not exceeding 200 watts and for a voltage exceeding 100 volts
67	8544.11–8544.59	Wires and cables
68	9032.89	Other automatic voltage stabilizer
69	9102.19	Pocket watches and wristwatches
70	9105.29	Wall clocks
71	9403.10–9403.90	Furniture, including metal and plastic furniture
72	9603.21	Toothbrushes, including dental plate brushes
73	9608.10	Ballpoint pen
74	6103.42	Men's or boys' trousers
75	6104.62	Women's or girls' trousers, overalls, and knitted-cotton shorts
76	6105.20	Men's or boys' shirts of synthetic fibers
77	6106.10	Women's or girls' blouses, shirts, and shirt-blouses of knitted cotton
78	6109.90	T-shirts, singlets, and other vests of other textile materials
79	6110.20	Sweaters, sweatshirts, and waistcoats of knitted cotton
80	6110.30	Sweaters, sweatshirts, and waistcoats knitted of synthetic fibers
81	6110.90	Sweaters, sweatshirts, and waistcoats knitted of other textile materials
82	6111.20	Sweaters, sweatshirts, and waistcoats knitted of cotton
83	6111.30	Sweaters, sweatshirts, and waistcoats knitted of synthetic fibers
84	6203.42	Men's and boys' trousers, overalls, and shorts of woven cotton
85	6203.43	Men's and boys' trousers, overalls, and shorts of woven synthetic fibers
86	6204.52	Women's and girls' skirts and divided skirts of woven cotton
87	6204.62	Women's and girls' trousers, overalls, and shorts of woven cotton
88	6205.20	Men's and boys' shirts of woven cotton
89	6205.30	Men's and boys' shirts of woven synthetic fibers
90	6206.30	Women's and girls' blouses, shirts, and shirt-blouses of woven cotton

HS = Harmonized System.

Source: Government of Bhutan and Government of India. 2016. *Agreement on Trade, Commerce and Transit between the Royal Government of Bhutan and the Government of the Republic of India*. Thimphu.

Table A4.3: Proposed List of 15 Products for Exemption of Customs Duty

Series No.	HS Code	Description of the Item
1.	7202.21.00	Ferrosilicon: containing by weight more than 55% silicon
2.	2201.10	Mineral waters and aerated waters
3.	2007.10–2007.99	Jams, fruit jellies, marmalades, fruit or nut puree, and fruit or nut pastes obtained by cooking, whether or not containing added sugar or other sweetening matter
4.	2523.21–2523.29	Portland cement
5.	7214.20	TMT bars and rods
6.	2523.10	Cement clinkers
7.	0410.20	UHT milk
8.	8309.90	Stoppers, caps, and lids (including crown corks, screw caps, and pouring stoppers); capsules for bottles; threaded bungs; bung covers; seals and other packing accessories, of base metal
9.	2516.90	Stone boulders
10.	2506.10–2506.20	Quartz (other than natural sands); quartzite, whether or not roughly trimmed or merely cut, by sawing or otherwise, into blocks or slabs of a rectangular (including square) shape
11.	9403.30–9403.90	Furniture
12.	1101.00	Wheat and meslin flour
13.	2302.30	Wheat bran
14.	0409.00	Natural honey
15.	4410.11–4410.90	Particle board, oriented standard board, and similar board (for example, oriented strand board and waferboard) of wood or other ligneous materials, whether or not agglomerated with resins or other organic binding substances

HS = Harmonized System, TMT = thermo-mechanical treatment, UHT = ultra-high temperature.
Source: Government of Bhutan and Government of India. 2016. *Agreement on Trade, Commerce and Transit between the Royal Government of Bhutan and the Government of the Republic of India*. Thimphu.

Table A4.4: Additional Products for Exemption of Customs Duty

Series No.	HS Code	Description of the Item
1.	3401.11–3401.20	Soap for toilet use, soap in other forms
2.	2106.10.00	Protein concentrates and textured protein substances
3.	2304.00.00	Oil-cake and other solid residues, whether or not ground or in the form of pellets, resulting from the extraction of soybean oil
4.	2308.00.00	Vegetable materials and vegetable waste, vegetable residues and by-products, whether or not in the form of pellets, of a kind used in animal feeding, not elsewhere specified or included

HS = Harmonized System.
Source: Government of Bhutan and Government of India. 2016. *Agreement on Trade, Commerce and Transit between the Royal Government of Bhutan and the Government of the Republic of India*. Thimphu.

Appendix 5
Stakeholders and Contributors to the Bhutan National Diagnostic Study

Ministry of Agriculture and Forests

Bhutan Agriculture Food and Regulatory Authority

Namgay Wangchuk	Director general
Chador Wangdi	Chief regulatory and quarantine officer
Jamyang Phuntsho	Chief, analytical and certification division
Jambay Dorji	In-charge officer, National Food Testing Laboratory, Yusipang
Gyem Bedha	Focal officer for food section
Sonam Dorji	Focal officer for plant section, Quarantine Division
Yeshi Wangchuk	Senior regulatory and quarantine officer, Phuentsholing
Kinzang Gyaltshen	Regulatory and quarantine officer, Phuentsholing
Karma Yangzome	Senior regulatory and quarantine officer
Gyem Bidha	Senior regulatory and quarantine officer
Sonam Yangden	Laboratory Technician, Phuentsholing
Prakash Tamang	Regulatory and quarantine officer
Kubrinath	Regulatory and quarantine officer
Sonam Deki	Regulatory and quarantine officer
Yeshi Lham	Regulatory and quarantine officer

National Plant Protection Center

Saha Bir Rai	Senior plant protection officer
Tsheltrim Zangpo	Plant protection officer
Pema Thinley	Plant protection officer
Thinley	Plant protection specialist
Rieks van Klinken	Avid advisor

Department of Agriculture Marketing and Cooperatives

Ugyen Penjor	Director general
Yonten Gyamtsho	Chief marketing officer
Tshewang Norbu	Marketing officer

Department of Livestock

DhanRai	Program director, National Diary Research Center
M.P Thimsina	Specialist, National Diary Research Center
Sonam Chedup	Farm manager, Farrowing Unit, National Piggery Research Center
Choedup Gyaltshen	Farm manager, Regional Pig Breeding Center
Sonam Norbu	Livestock production officer

Bhutan Standards Bureau

Sonam Phuntsho	Director general
Tashi Wangchuk	Official deputy to South Asian Regional Standards Organization
Tshering Tashi	Head, Standardization Division
Tenzin Dorji	Head, Metrology Division
Nidup Dorji	Deputy executive engineer, Metrology Division
Leki Choden	Metrology Laboratory In-Charge
Tenzin Dorji	Chief engineer, Metrology Division
Karma Wangdi	Chief engineer, Certification Division
Tashi Yuden	Laboratory technician, Metrology Laboratory
Tandin Choden	Laboratory technician, Metrology Laboratory
Karma Wangdi	International Relations Division
Karma Tshetrim	Standardization Division
Tashi Choden	Standardization Division
Tashi Tenzin	Assistant research officer, Standardization Division
Tenzin Dorji	Metrology Division
Nidup Dorji	Metrology Division

Ministry of Finance

Department of Revenue and Customs

Kinzang Wangdi	Joint commissioner, regional office
Yeshi Dorji	Senior revenue officer

Ministry of Economic Affairs

Department of Trade

Sonam Tenzin	Director
Pem Bedha	Regional director, Regional Trade Office
Chimi Tshering	Chief, Trade Promotion Division
Zecko Dukpa	Chief, Export Promotion Division
Kinley Yangzome	Deputy chief trade officer, Export Promotion Division
Dechen Zam	Trade officer, Export Promotion Division

Department of Industry

Loknath Chapagai — Specialist

Bhutan Chamber of Commerce and Industry

Phub Tshering	Secretary general
Kesang Wangdi	Deputy secretary general
Tandin Wangchuk	Vice president
Sangay Dorji	Bhutan Chamber of Commerce and Industry, Phuentsholing

Bhutan Exporters Association

Tshering Yeshi — General secretary

Association of Bhutanese Industries

Jochu Dukpa — General secretary

Private Sector Companies

Tikka Sharun	Executive director, RSA Private Limited, RSA Group of Companies (gypsum, plastics, boulders, cardamom, oranges)
Singye Namgay	Managing director, RSA Private Limited, RSA Group of Companies (gypsum, plastics, boulders, cardamom, oranges)
Karma Dorji	Managing director, Karma Group of Companies (animal feeds, steel, ingots)
Kenchok Wangdi	Director, production and sales, Karma Group of Companies (animal feeds, steel, ingots)
Rajiv Miahra	Executive director, Pelden Group of Companies (steel and ferrosilicon)
Aum Damchae Dem	Chair, Pelden Group of Companies (steel and ferrosilicon)
Niladri Bose	Head, marketing department, Pelden Group of Companies (steel and ferrosilicon)
Subhendu Kundu	General manager, finance, Pelden Group of Companies (steel and ferrosilicon)
Arun Gupta	Manager, finance department, Zimdra Group (processed fruit juice and Tetra Pack ultra-high temperature milk)
Namgay Chencho	Liaison officer and human resources officer, Zimdra Group (processed fruit juice and Tetra Pack ultra-high temperature milk)
Gyem Dorji	Managing director, Bhutan Agro Industries Limited
Tashi Wangdi	Marketing manager, Bhutan Agro Industries Limited

Tshering Dorji	Proprietor, Bitumen Emulsion
Prakasan Nair	General manager, marketing, Bitumen Emulsion
Dilip Chhetri	Senior manager, sales and purchase, Bhutan Carbide Chemicals Limited
Chencho Norbu	Senior marketing manager, Bhutan Carbide Chemicals Limited
Kishore Gurung	Senior manager, purchase of stores and spares, Bhutan Carbide Chemicals Limited
S.N Goldier	Senior general manager, Corporate Division, Bhutan Ferro Alloys Private Limited
Jeevan Kafley	Senior manager, Marketing Division, Bhutan Ferro Alloys Private Limited
Samdrup Dorji	Manager, Marketing Division, Bhutan Silica Metal
Kinley Dorji	Manager, marketing and sales, Bhutan Brewery Private Limited
Sonam Wangchuk	General manager, Bhutan Particle Board Private Limited
Nagendra Sharma	Manager, personnel and administration, Bhutan Particle Board Private Limited
Narendra Rai	Deputy general manager, marketing and sales, Bhutan Particle Board Private Limited
Satyam Gurung	General manager, Yarab Cables Private Limited
S.K. Tarafdar	Manager, finance and accounts and procurement, Dralha Flour Mills
Shamshar Alam	Sales and Marketing Division, Dralha Flour Mills
Bhim Gurung	Technical advisor, Food Corporation of Bhutan
Tshering Dorji	Marketing officer, Food Corporation of Bhutan

References

I. Cheong, T. Bark, and H. Y. Jeong. 2015. A Framework of Trade Policy for Bhutan: Compatible with Gross National Happiness. *ADB South Asia Working Paper Series*. No. 39. Manila: Asian Development Bank.

Food and Agriculture Organization of the United Nations and Government of Bhutan. 2012. *Strengthening Food Safety and Standards in Bhutan*. Rome.

Government of Bangladesh, Bangladesh Customs. *Bangladesh Customs National Tariff: Fiscal Year 2016–2017*.

Government of Bhutan, Bhutan Standards Bureau. Unpublished. Draft National Quality Policy.

Government of Bhutan, Ministry of Agriculture and Forests. 2015. *Bhutan RNR Statistics 2015*. Thimphu.

———. *National Food Testing Laboratory Progress Report, January–March 2016*. Thimphu.

———. 2015. *Gist of Achievements August 2000–June 2014*. Thimphu.

———. *National Food Act of Bhutan, 2005*. Thimphu.

———. *The Plant Quarantine Act of Bhutan, 1993*. Thimphu.

Government of Bhutan, Royal Monetary Authority. 2017. *Annual Report of Royal Monetary Authority of Bhutan, 2015–2016*. Thimphu.

Government of Bhutan and Government of Bangladesh. 2014A. *Agreement on Trade between the Royal Government of Bhutan and the Government of the People's Republic of Bangladesh*. Dhaka.

———. 2014B. *Protocol to the Agreement on Trade between the Royal Government of Bhutan and the Government of the People's Republic of Bangladesh*. Dhaka.

Government of Bhutan and Government of India. 2016. *Agreement on Trade, Commerce and Transit between the Royal Government of Bhutan and the Government of the Republic of India*. Thimphu.

Government of India, Ministry of Finance, Department of Revenue. Central Board of Indirect Taxes and Customs.

S. Raihan, M.A. Khan, and S. Quoreshi. 2014. *NTMs in South Asia: Assessment and Analysis*. Kathmandu: South Asian Association for Regional Cooperation Trade Promotion Network.

www.ingramcontent.com/pod-product-compliance
Lightning Source LLC
Chambersburg PA
CBHW040547220526
45473CB00017B/3042